Go Beyond Your Dreams

(Live Them!)

By: Farrell Ellis

Copyright © 2009

Farrell Ellis for McClure Publishing, Inc.

All rights reserved. Printed and bound in the United States of America. According to the 1976 United States Copyright Act, no part of this book may be reproduced or utilized in any form or by any means, electronic or mechanical, including photocopying, recording, or by any information storage or retrieval system, except by a reviewer who may quote brief passages in a review to be printed in a magazine or newspaper, without permission in writing from the Publisher: Inquiries should be addressed to McClure Publishing, Inc. Permissions Department, 9624 S. Cicero, #175, Oak Lawn, Illinois 60453. First Printing: February 7, 2009.

Unless otherwise indicated, all scripture quotation indicated (AMP) are taken from The Amplified Bible, Old Testament copyright © 1965, 1987, by the Zondervan Corporation. The Amplified New Testament copyright © 1958, 1987 by the Lockman Foundation. Used by permission. Scripture quotations indicated (THE MESSAGE) are taken from THE MESSAGE. Copyright © 1994, 1995, 1996, 2000, 2001, 2002. Used by permission of NavPress Publishing Group. All references to satan are purposely lower cased, because we give no credit to satan.

The author and publisher have made every effort to ensure the accuracy and completeness of information contained in this book, we assume no responsibility for errors, inaccuracies, omissions, or any inconsistency therein. Any slights of people, places, belief systems or organizations are unintentional. Any resemblance to anyone living, dead or somewhere in between is truly coincidental.

ISBN-13: 978-0-9790450-5-9
ISBN-10: 0-9790450-5-3
LCCN: 2008944267

Cover Art by Gabriel Peak

To order additional copies, please contact:
McClure Publishing, Inc.
www.mcclurepublishing.com
800.659.4908
mcclurepublishing@msn.com

My Voice...
There are, it may be, so many kinds of voices in the world and none of them is without signification. (KJV)
I Corinthians 14:10

My Instruction...
The Lord gives the word [of power]; the women who bear and publish [the news] are a great host. (AMP)
Psalms 68:11

My Reward...
[Jesus said], "Everything is possible for him who believes." (NIV)
Mark 9:23

Acknowledgement

I'm grateful for the precious gift of writing. I thank God for inspiring me from a young girl to write from my heart! I want to thank my wonderful family. Avery, Renee and Jeannette, you've been there to encourage me every step of the way. You have given me a lot of support with this dream of mine for as long as I can remember first sharing it with you. I also want to acknowledge my nephew Andrew, and my nieces Fredreca and Alexis. I love each of you so very much! I'd also like to recognize my Pastor, Kenneth E. Gaines and his lovely wife, First Lady Renae. He brings the Word of God in a simplistic way that I can understand and apply to my life on a needed daily basis. My Pastor prophesied seven years ago that there was a book inside of me. I received that prophetic word in my spirit, and refused to let it go! Today that prophecy has manifested in my life!

Dedication

This book is dedicated to two very special people, my mother, Levoular Smith, who went home to be with the Lord, July 2008, and my brother, Dezret Smith who preceded her, August 2003. I miss them both so much! However, I'm comforted knowing I shall see them again one day! I love you, mom and Dez!

Go Beyond Your Dreams
Chapter Contents

CHAPTER 1 17
  God Wants You To Be Prosperous

CHAPTER 2 31
  If You Can Believe It, You Can Achieve It

CHAPTER 3 57
  You Are Blessed

CHAPTER 4 75
  Do Not Be Moved

CHAPTER 5 91
  The Promises of God Are Meant For You

CHAPTER 6 97
  Trust In God's Unfailing Love

CHAPTER 7 125
  Depending On The Wisdom of God

CHAPTER 8 141
  Show God You're Trustworthy

CHAPTER 9 155
  What's Inside Your Heart

CHAPTER 10 167
  Peace of Mind Is A Necessity

CHAPTER 11 183
    Live In Peace With Your Prosperity

CONCLUSION 193
    Go Beyond Your Dreams!

SALVATION (A MIRACLE) AWAITS YOU! 201

ABBREVIATION REFERENCE BOOKS OF THE
    BIBLE 205

Let Me Introduce Myself

"Hello!" You already know my name, so you have me at an advantage. If you're accustomed to a straight-laced nonfiction writer, you're not going to find that here. I'll be conversing with you the way I normally do with my closest girlfriends. And, hopefully if I'm well received, I'll continue writing more books after this one. Pray for me girl!

This book is going to be down-to-earth because that's who I am. I ride the bus five days a week to get to and from work. I pack lunch to save money because I'm a bargain shopper. I'm fifty something, look like I'm thirty something, and that's enough of that!

I love my closest girlfriends, and I try to fellowship with them for lunch, dinner, movies or get-away Caribbean vacations whenever our schedules permit. We are busy pursuing our God-given passions. My God-given passion for writing is obvious. What you don't know about me is how much I love the Lord! But you will, by the time you finish reading this book. Well, enough about me; very nice to meet you. Hopefully, one day in the near future we'll meet in person, possibly at a book signing. It seems as if I met you already. Nice meeting you, girl!

The vision for writing *Go Beyond Your Dreams* was part of an unforeseen spiritual makeover. I couldn't see it at the time because I was experiencing problems in my marriage. But God had a plan. While writing this book, I realized I was opening myself up to strangers, which is normally out of character for me. I'm more of a private person. As a child my mother raised my siblings and I to be closed mouth children. We didn't blab to our neighbors what went on inside of our house. This kind of rearing has always stayed with me. Therefore, I'm limited on how much I tell people about me, or what's going on in my personal life. But writing this book was different. After all, how could I possibly write something I didn't believe myself, yet expect the text to be believed by someone else? The answer was rather simple. Unless I shared my experiences, I'd be of little, or probably no help at all, and that would defeat the entire purpose for writing in the first place. So I don't have a problem with telling you about some of the stuff I've gone through, if it means helping you to avoid some of those same experiences.

Three years ago, I began preparing myself for what I thought was going to be a brief marital separation. Out of despair and loneliness, one night I telephoned my closest friend, Jeannette. She and I have been through a lot together. I think of her more like having another sister. *"Girl,"* I said into the phone trying not to cry. *"I don't know how much longer this marriage is going to last. It's not looking too good."* Many times she gives it to me straight, just the way I need it. That's why she's been my best friend since we were children. True friends don't hold back. I've always appreciated her loyalty and honesty.

Recently she'd been having a few problems herself. Jeannette was feeling slightly dismayed that plans weren't going quite the way she had imagined they'd be. She and I are Christian women. We know what the Word of God says. Nevertheless, we're not immune from discouragement creeping into our lives. We are still human. Following our lengthy phone conversation we prayed together before hanging up. As I laid the cordless phone down in the cradle, I determined within myself, I wasn't going to shrink back spiritually. During this rocky period in my marriage I turned to my Bible. I've always read the Bible, but lacked the discipline to make reading it a part of my daily life. I began praying more frequently. I'd get alone inside the bedroom where I could praise and worship God to the top of my lungs if I wished.

Then God began revealing to me through His Word, that if I would put *all* of my faith in Him, He wouldn't let me fail. Suddenly it made perfect sense to stretch my faith like I never had before! I'm not exaggerating when I tell you as I prepared to strengthen my heart in faith, everything I wanted or needed in my husband's absence, God supplied the need! I'll admit. There were times when some of the problems in my marriage came to such a boil, that I was tempted to turn away from God. But something deep down on the inside of me wouldn't allow me to give up. Even in my temporary state of confusion, a part of me needed to lean on God.

Now that I'm a little older in my Christian walk, I understand the discord within my marriage was part of a devious plan to make me fall apart spiritually. The enemy (satan) wanted me to give up on the validity of God's Word. I'm pretty sure I would've sank into a state of depression had the enemy succeeded in persuading me to take my eyes off God. I certainly wouldn't have written this book! After all, I needed God's Word flowing in my heart to help defuse those crazy thoughts that kept popping up inside my head. The more I read the Bible my hearing grew dull to the hissing lies of the devil. It was imperative for me to understand that no matter what happened in my marriage, God was still in control! I soon got my mind in line with God's Word. If I was going to overcome my situation without so much as a mental scratch, I had to believe with all of my heart that God was able to get me through this rough period, regardless how things were looking at that particular moment. I had to believe He was going to turn things around for me.

One night before crawling into bed I asked God, *"what must I do to keep my faith from being shaken?"* I laid there waiting for an answer, but when I hadn't heard anything by 1:00 a.m., I went to sleep. A couple of days later, I was sitting in the kitchen at the table. It was a drag sitting there trying to figure out which bill wasn't getting paid so I'd have enough money to pay the mortgage. That's when I received my answer. God will meet you wherever you are. He met me in the privacy of my kitchen that morning. Sitting at the kitchen table, I was reminded to believe my prayers had already been answered.

Girlfriend, even though I heard those words in my spirit, I was still concerned about the mortgage getting paid, but faith has to start somewhere. My financial situation opened my eyes. I hungered to learn more about the faith God speaks of in the Bible. I wanted to saturate my heart with the kind of faith that Jesus said would move mountains. I'd been hoping the bills would get paid, but it was going to take more than hope. It was going to take a heart of strong faith to make certain they were paid. As I read scriptures and studied my Bible, I slowly began to comprehend if I was going to possess a genuine heart filled with faith, I couldn't let what was going on around me, consume me.

Once I finally grabbed hold of that revelation, I dared not let it go! But it would take a well thought out plan to keep me on track. I'll elaborate on that later in the book. Sad to say, my marriage dissolved the following winter. I couldn't see it then, but my future was under construction. However, instead of feeling sorry for myself, I turned to my computer. I vividly recall it was on a Saturday afternoon when God gave me the idea for this book. I began channeling all of my energy into writing. It seemed the more pages I wrote, the more my emotional hurt, anger and disappointment seemed to fade away.

Between reading God's Word and working on this book, I had a revelation. Before God could begin healing my brokenness, I had to *do* something. God was waiting on me to completely trust Him. He was waiting for me to place all of my faith in Him. Upon releasing my trust and faith, God showed up on my behalf in a mighty powerful way. I was learning through the Word that His desire for me was to lead a whole, spirit-filled prosperous life!

Nine months prior to my husband moving out, I didn't have a clue I'd be responsible for paying a mortgage, the electric, maintaining my car note, and not to mention pay all the other bills. Without the financial support of my husband's income, how was I suppose to do this? We created a number of bills together. But you know what? God is faithful! I can earnestly say it was God who kept the bill collectors away. Through faith I managed to pay (on time) a hefty mortgage every month, including household utilities and other miscellaneous bills. Through faith I still paid my tithes. I bought groceries and had money left over after each paycheck! Miracles are real! Beyond my understanding I was doing more with less money! Girlfriend, there's no other way to explain what was happening with my finances, except to say, "*To God be the glory!*" Who couldn't trust a man like Him? Well, it's three years later and my broken heart has healed. I have a new lease on life. With God's help, I've blossomed into a confident Christian woman. I'm a living testimony! If God could turn my circumstances around, I know He can do the same for you! Let me tell you something. God doesn't play favorites. In His eyes all of His daughters are equal. By the time I completed writing this book, not only had I grown spiritually, but my life has changed for the better. I'm now motivated to pursue long lost dreams. Fear can no longer stop me from taking authority over negative situations. I'll always believe (by faith), a successful and prosperous lifestyle is available for me. And, you know what? It's available for you too!

Chapter 1
God Wants You To Be Prosperous

Let those who favor my righteous cause and have pleasure in my uprightness shout for joy and be glad and say continually, Let the Lord be magnified, Who takes pleasure in the prosperity of His servant. (AMP)

Psalms 35:27

God wants us to lead a prosperous lifestyle. He wants to see our body free from sicknesses to enjoy it. Divine health and the wealth of God belong to us! I'm not being silly. I realize within the large population of women we have to work, until we recognize our full potential. I also understand what happens if we ignore our medication. I'm simply trying to stress a point. God wants all of us to live in divine health, prosperity, and joy.

III John 2 reads:

> **Beloved, I pray that you may prosper in every way and [that your body] may keep you well, even as [I know] your soul keeps well *and* prospers. (AMP)**

I'd like to talk to you about possessing faith for prosperous living. Real faith serves as a tool which encourages us spiritually. In the scheme of things, the enemy wants to try to discourage us by injecting fear into us. He likes seeing us sick. He gets a kick out of watching us live paycheck-to-paycheck. God desires to see us living in divine health. The enemy wants to inflict our bodies with all sorts of infirmities. Why? Because the enemy's number one goal is to cause us to become too sick to enjoy the blessings of God. The enemy also would have us believe we cannot do any better than what we're doing right now. He purposely comes on the scene (usually at the worse times) to destroy our faith! The enemy plays mind games. He plants negative thoughts inside our heads. Then he sits back waiting to see if we'll entertain those thoughts. The enemy wants to stop us from comprehending the truth of God! Girlfriend, turn a deaf ear to any negative thoughts that enter your mind, because they will, and they do interfere with learning the truth about God's Word.

John 10:10 reads:

> **The thief comes only in order to steal and kill and destroy. I came that they may have *and* enjoy life, and have it in abundance (to the full, till it overflows). (AMP)**

It's God's will to see His daughters living healthy, abundant lives. God desires to see faith move us beyond anything we might ever imagine for ourselves. That in itself is very powerful! God wants

Go Beyond Your Dreams
(Live Them!)

us to dream big! Whether we know it, or not, the power of God works from within to assist us in accomplishing our goals. We've got the right stuff, baby! Everything we need (spiritually) to bring our dreams to pass is already built on the inside of us. (Deut. 8:18) Don't be afraid to step aside. Allow God to work through you.

Whenever we hear the word prosperity, naturally we associate it with having lots of money. But that's only part of it. Prosperity also means divine health in our body. When you think about it under those terms, be grateful that you woke up with a stable mind. The enemy never stops trying to take over our minds. When we can climb out of bed free from any bodily ailments, take it from me, that's a blessing! Prosperity can be moving out of a small, cramped apartment into a spacious new home. It could mean a promotion on our job, which ultimately will lead to debt freedom. God not only wants His daughters to live out our dreams, He wants us in excellent health so we can enjoy every good thing He pre-destined for our lives while we're in the earth. All God asks is that we live obedient to His Word.

As daughters of God, we're blessed. Why wouldn't we want to allow Him to fulfill the plans He has for us? The plans God has for our lives will always be insurmountable to anything we might ever plan. Do you know the moment you pray; you have what you prayed for right then in the spirit realm? However, we will be required to show God how much we believe in His Word by demonstrating what's in our heart.

Mark 11:24 reads:

> **That's why I urge you to pray for absolutely everything, ranging from small to large. Include everything as you embrace this God-life, and you'll get God's everything.** (THE MESSAGE)

For the most part, I'll be talking about achieving financial success through our visions and dreams. Girlfriend, once we grab hold of what God says about prosperity, we'll have to learn to ignore what other people might say. You know why? Because people will always say whatever they want to say! If we're doing badly, they have something to say about that. If we're doing well, they have something to say about that, too! Just because we would like to have more money at the end of the month doesn't suddenly mean we desire to have all the money in the world. Prepare yourself. The decision to step out of our comfortable surroundings causes people around us to start getting nervous! They're afraid this new change in our thought pattern just might propel us into our destiny. And, where would that leave them? Strangely enough, probably right where we last saw them.

As I mentioned, prosperity means different things for each of us. What does it mean for you? Ponder over that question for a minute. Then I

Go Beyond Your Dreams
(Live Them!)

challenge you to search within yourself. Seek God for answers. If we are women with dreams, He will reveal the plans He has placed within our hearts to bring it forth. Read God's Word for instructions. It's also a valuable asset to speak God's Word over our lives, and the lives of our loved ones. Speaking negative words over our families, our finances, and our health isn't using wisdom. Girlfriend, I'm not going to pretend every word that falls out of my mouth oozes with godliness. But I will tell you this. What we say can work for us, or against us.

    I can recall a time when I was growing up; my mother didn't have to be bothered with paying any bills. My father paid all of them. If something in our house broke down, my father fixed it. Daddy was definitely the head of his household. My father was the disciplinary and the provider. My mother was his helpmate. She was a stay at home mom, which I loved. At age fifteen my father passed away. Shortly after dad died, I watched the enemy try to steal my mother's voice. Within a couple of weeks following my dad's death, she couldn't speak above a whisper. When the enemy couldn't succeed at keeping her quiet, he switched gears. He then tried suppressing a longing in her heart to work outside the home. I watched him bring people into my mother's life who meant her no good. My mother was thirty-four years young. I'm sure she missed my father.

    But God is good! Roughly about a year later my mother did a three hundred and sixty degree turn.

She started a daycare in our home. Four years later she began working in the school system. I guess you could say my mother discovered her calling. I'm not saying this because she's my mother, but my mom was a wonderful teacher! I should've known there was a reason why she was always insisting that my siblings and I *"get somewhere and read a book!"* When she set her sights on college, the enemy tried to discourage her. He planted the idea of being too old.

I was in my second year of college at the time. I thought it was cool my mother wanted to further her education. Naturally, I encouraged her to go. My mother and I attended the same college. We even graduated together. Over the years mother found her calling in educating children from various backgrounds and all ages. She taught children under, and up to five years of age. In her passion for educating pre-*schoolers*, my mother found it self-rewarding. She was prosperous in her career many times over. So you see, prosperity is what you make it. It's not always about dollars and cents.

In many ways my mother was a very prosperous woman. She celebrated her seventy-second birthday in December 2007. In 2006 she was honored along with three other women to be spiritual mothers for our church. My mother was my hero. She overcame a lot of adversity. My mother was an example for me. By putting her trust in God, and His Word, she was able to lead a full rewarding life! And,

Go Beyond Your Dreams
(Live Them!)

while she is no longer here with me, I thank God for her everyday. I love you, mom!

Today, a large majority of women are raising children alone. Often times within six weeks of giving birth, most women are forced to put their newborn babies in daycare because they must return to work. A lot of women have become the bread winners in their families. They oversee that all the bills are paid. When something breaks down in their home they have to find a repairman in the yellow pages. Some women practically have to beg their employer to allow them time off to pick a sick child up from school, or daycare. And, if the employer does let her leave, more times than not she has to make up the time missed. I don't have any children. But I'd like to take a moment to salute mothers everywhere!

If you're a working woman, you know in the work place we absorb just as much pressure as the men. Usually we're paid less, and probably work harder than most men. But praise God anyhow! I suspect men are paid more than women because after all, *they are supposed to be the head over their household.* Unfortunately, changing times have proved hardworking family men have fallen prey to the hands of the enemy. Too many men are missing from the home. But girlfriend, the absence of a man in the home isn't the end of the world. Everything that the enemy does for a woman's demise, God can turn it around to her advantage. In the meantime, there is something we can do to avoid the pitfalls of ill health, and living paycheck-to-paycheck.

Deuteronomy 28:1 and 28:9 reads:

> **If you listen obediently to the Voice of God, your God, and heartily obey all his commandments that I command you today, God your God, will place you on high above all the nations of the world.**
>
> **God will form you as a people holy to him, just as he promised you, if you keep the commandments of God, your God, and live the way he has shown you.** (THE MESSAGE)

One of the keys to obtaining God's kind of success requires obedience to His Word. The repercussions of disobedience are very costly. Not only does it cost us spiritually, it can cost us our very souls. Plenty of times when I've gone up against the world, acting out of my flesh, I reaped a lot of unnecessary heartache and despair. Girlfriend, when we refuse to accept the instructions of God, hardships fall upon us. Disobedience opens the door for the enemy. When acting out of disobedience, things we set out to accomplish usually don't work out very well. Actually, little or nothing goes in our favor when we fail to follow God's Word of instructions. Let me ask you something. Have you noticed over the last 20 years there are a lot of very successful

Go Beyond Your Dreams (Live Them!)

women in this country? Some are CEO's of giant companies. There are women with large ministries spreading the Gospel. We have women on TV with talk shows. Female baby boomers have populated the once dominated political male arena. And, let's not overlook the women who juggle both family and careers. Baby, we have come a long way! And, having said that, please do not allow yourself to become easily discourage by the condition(s) of your present circumstance. Clearly, we all need to rely on faith. God's Word tells us through faith we are made spiritually strong. Girlfriend, there are no failures in God! Stay focused! While you're waiting for the manifestations of what you're believing God to do in your life, don't stress yourself! Every time you pray from a grateful heart, God hears you! Therefore, whenever you decree (pray) a thing, believe it will be established unto you.

Job 22:25-28 reads:

> **Relax your grip on money and abandon your gold-plated luxury. God Almighty will be your treasure, more wealth than you can imagine. You'll take delight in God, the Mighty One, and look to him joyfully, boldly. You'll pray to him and he'll listen; he'll help you do what you've promised. You'll decide what you want and it will happen; your life will be bathed in light.** (THE MESSAGE)

I want to touch on something that often rears its ugly head when others see you taking yourself seriously. You may as well know that a prospering lifestyle may not go over very well with other females. I'm referring to the spirit of jealousy. Sorry girls, but you know how we can get! So, the next time you recognize jealousy staring back at you, I want you to do something for me. I want you to ask yourself. Who are *they* to put limitations on my prosperity? Have *they* seen what I give in tithes and offerings? Do *they* know the sacrifices I've made? Do *they* know how often I fellowship with God in prayer, praise and worship? Have *they* seen the long suffering behind my diligence? By the way girlfriend, who are *they* anyhow? You know what irks me about people? It's always a *they* brought into a conversation. It's never *them* talking about you behind your back. It's always *they* said it. Please will someone tell me who *they* are? The worse thing you can do is start getting all freaked out by what *they* have to say about your faith for *your* dreams! I read in the book of Ecclesiastes (Ecc. 5:9), the profit of the earth is for everyone. That sounds like there's plenty of prosperity available for *them* too!

Now this is where things might get a little touchy-feely. But I'm only telling you this because I had to learn the hard way. Don't be naïve like I was. Everybody isn't going to be happy about you wanting to pursue a dream. People will try to convince you it's okay to go through life with a little bit of this, and

Go Beyond Your Dreams
(Live Them!)

even less of that. This is a cleverly disguised voice of deception talking from the enemy. It's aimed at keeping you trapped in a poverty mindset. It's uniquely designed to make you feel guilty for even having a dream. But we cannot allow ourselves to be held hostage by the opinions of others. And that goes for me too! My friend that's people bondage! We mustn't give anyone permission to disconnect us from our faith. The prosperity of God belongs to you! I repeat. It belongs to you!

You have the ability to bring forth prosperity when you receive the Word of God into your heart. In reading the Bible, I discovered God speaks of prospering in every area of our lives. He isn't just talking about m-o-n-e-y. God is also talking about possessing good health, peace, joy, blessings that money cannot buy, and successes in things that money cannot begin to buy! However, in all of our possessing, there's also a need for grace (God's unmerited favor) while pursuing visions and dreams. God's grace helps to sustain us in the midst of everything going on around us. I won't hide the fact that once your mind is made up to increase faith that produces results, your life will probably get a little crazy. You could come under attack by anything, or from anyone. But thank God, He deposits grace into our lives so that we're able to endure those moments. It won't be easy building your heart in faith, but the more you hear God's Word, read His Word, and believe what you're reading and hearing, it softens your heart to receive. A receptive heart will grow stronger, thereby raising your level of faith. Make no mistake about it. Women need faith! We need it for our children. We need it for our husbands. We need faith for our jobs. We need it for our schools, and our churches. Let's face it. We need faith for everything!

In the book of Hebrews we're told without faith it is impossible to please God. (Heb. 11:6) Faith is God's promise that if we can believe out of a genuine heart, we can receive the desires of our heart. It really doesn't matter what anyone else may say, or think. The only thing that matters most is what God says. And, He says our visions and dreams can come to pass!

Everything I've written so far has been based on three steps to achieve the success God has planned and purposed for you. **<u>First,</u>** stop procrastinating. An act of procrastination is only fear trying to keep you right where you are. (Jn. 10:10) **<u>Second,</u>** write your vision down. (Hab. 2:2) **<u>Third,</u>** keep dreaming bigger than you ever have before! Once you've accomplished steps 1, 2, and 3 of these spiritual aerobics, move forward by taking the limits off God!

Let me ask you something. When you pray, are you specific? If so, your vision should be written down in detail. After you've written it down, I challenge you to either find magazine pictures or photographs of that vision. Then I want you to tape the picture(s) wherever you'll see it everyday. I have pictures in my bathroom and my bedroom. I also

Go Beyond Your Dreams
(Live Them!)

bought myself a binder where I keep pictures for everything I see myself possessing in the near future. Since I'm sharing, I'll let you in on something else. I'm so sure these spiritual aerobic exercises will work for you that if they didn't, you wouldn't be reading this book. I would never have written it. Early on I had to come to the realization that if I wanted to see positive changes taking place in my life, I had to learn to trust God at His Word.

I began reading the Bible for one hour every night. I'm not a morning person. I exercise at night. But be that as it may, what you see here girlfriend is living proof that faith really works! Now, you may ask yourself, *"Why should I bother doing any of this?"* Well, have you ever heard the old saying, "out of sight, out of mind?" That's pretty much how it works for a vision too. If you can't actually see yourself doing this particular thing, then it certainly won't have much of an impression on your mind. A dream must start with reprogramming your thought process. I imagine you're probably thinking, okay now what? Well girlfriend, here comes the part that moves steps 1, 2 and 3 into motion to bring those dreams to fruition. Are you up for the challenge?

What you and I must always keep in the back of our minds is the fact that God isn't a respecter of people. What He did for one, He'll do for another. Stop telling yourself that there's no way you can be a successful business woman, owning and operating your very own hair salon. Stop telling yourself you can never go back to college for your Master's Degree. We girls have to stop letting the enemy have his way over our minds. He's a liar! The truth isn't in him! Satan lied to Eve. He's been lying to females ever since! I don't care if your desire is something intangible, God says you can have whatsoever you desire! As I mentioned before, success is personal. It's what you make it. No two women are going to have the exact same dreams or visions because God isn't into duplicating. We're all different because it was His plan and purpose to single each one of us out as individuals. You must seek God for divine direction, for clarity, and insight into His plans and purpose for you here in the earth. If you begin to make the time for Him, God will show up and show out in ways you never thought possible!

Chapter 2
If You Can Believe It, You Can Achieve It

And whatever you ask for in prayer, having faith and [really] believing you will receive. (AMP)

Matthew 21:22

It's time for more spiritual aerobic exercises. To achieve anything it must start with building up on faith. The possession of a strong, God kind of faith does produce results. The God kind of faith has to obey you. I can imagine that probably sounds like quite a statement. But it's the truth.

Luke 17:6 reads:

> **And the Lord answered, If you had faith (trust and confidence in God) even [so small] like a grain of mustard seed, you could say to this mulberry tree, Be pulled up by the roots, and be planted in the sea, and it would obey you.** (AMP)

However, there is a 'but' clause. *But you can't be double-minded.* You can't be in church on Sunday agreeing with everything your pastor preaches, keeping a seat warm. Then come Monday you speak something completely the opposite of what you agreed to just yesterday. We've all done it, so no surprise there. The thing is. Girlfriend, if you've got the heart of a doubting Thomasina, you need not expect God to move on your behalf. How can He, if you really don't believe you have what it takes to make your dreams come true?

In the book of Genesis there are nine verses in the very first chapter that begin with... ***"and God said."*** Those three words magnify manifestation. We learn from our Heavenly Father by speaking out in faith, a vision *can* and *does* produce results! God created the heavens and the earth by speaking out what He envisioned for all of mankind. God demonstrated what can happen when we have heart-filled faith.

From one woman to another, I certainly understand how emotional issues often prevent a large majority of us from pursuing visions that God has given us. We've all dealt with some kind of drama at one time or another. Drama seems to be a female fact of life. Then again, women are known for being drama queens. Now, let's move on, shall we? Most issues are self-inflicted. They are little fears we inflict upon ourselves. Do you know one of the hindrances to your faith is that dreadful woulda-shoulda-coulda spirit? Indecisiveness hinders your faith. The best thing you can do is release any type of negativity that leads you to doubt yourself.

Go Beyond Your Dreams
(Live Them!)

I'd like to share a story with you about a certain woman in the Bible. This woman tolerated an annoying issue for several years. She sought the help of doctors. But the only thing they were able to do was put a temporary band-aid on her problem. This woman longed to be free of this issue. My guess is, she must've felt very much alone. She was none other than the woman with the issue of blood. (Matt. 9:20-22) (Mk. 5:24-34) (Lk. 8:43-48)

The reason I use this illustration is because in spite of her circumstances, this woman had a vision. It didn't matter what her situation looked like. She cared even less what others had to say. This woman saw herself completely healed long before it ever happened. Day after day, week after week, month after month she believed for healing. Her faith intensified. There seem to be no one who understood her plight. The enemy did everything he could to discourage her from pursuing her dream to lead a healthy life. I've been there a few times myself.

During the eight years of my marriage there were certain issues that began tearing down the one thing I still had left—hope. Over time, unconsciously I began stroking my emotions of guilt, anger, and confusion. I have a shoe fetish. My closet isn't large enough to hold all the boxes, yet I keep buying shoes! Do you know a good shoe therapist? Anyway, at the time buying more pairs of shoes seemed to soothe my pain. Spiritually, I was restless day in and day out. Naturally, purchasing ten pairs of shoes at one time only jacked up my credit card! The natural (my flesh) side of me ignored my spiritual side when it advised me against buying those shoes on credit. And, while I am a spirit first and natural second, I have the will to listen to one or the other. We all do.

Those reoccurring issues in my marriage were draining me. Yet, I wanted to believe that somehow things would turn around for us. Sometimes I felt like I was the only woman on the planet going through an unstable marriage. Unresolved, burdensome issues can make a woman feel very alone. Whether she is being attacked physically, or under siege within her mind, these are a type of infirmity. Haunting issues can be mentally crippling. They taught me how to pretend all was right with the world. Instead of confronting them, I learned how to keep my problems on lock-down, when all I really wanted to do was scream! At times I was under so much emotional agony. I wanted to smack somebody! I mastered how to wear phony smiles. I even adopted this push-m-down-hold'm-back technique with my issues. But enough about me. Let's get back to the woman in the Bible.

She was told about a great man traveling from town to town. She heard He possessed the power to heal the sick of their infirmities. News was spreading quickly about this healing preacher man who called himself, Jesus. The woman heard reports how suddenly the deaf could hear. The cripple miraculously were walking. The blind received their sight. She knew without any doubt, she must meet this man for herself. If He was healing other people from their sicknesses, then she was certain He could heal her too. She believed! Determined to seek out this mighty man of power, she traveled to the town where Jesus was scheduled to preach the gospel. Upon her arrival to her surprise, there were hundreds of people smothered about the healer.

What takes place next clearly defines a genuine heart of faith. I wouldn't be surprised after seeing all those people if her mind didn't start playing tricks with her. That's how the enemy works. He plants negative thoughts in our minds hoping we'll forfeit what God has for us. If this woman hesitated, I suspect it was only for a second because she immediately dropped to her knees. What appeared to the natural eye as impossible to reach Jesus standing afar off, faith made possible within her heart. As she crawled through the crowd, she made this confession. According to Luke, she said it out loud *"If I can just touch the hem of his garment, I know I'll be healed*!"

It was an act of courageous faith that helped this woman crawl pass the feet of many people gathered about the healer. Suddenly she was within reach of His ankles. Her faith level intensified beyond anything she'd ever thought possible in the past. Within another inch of Jesus' ankles, she stretched forth her hand. Acting upon the faith stored inside her heart, she touched the hem of His clothing.

She believed she would live out the remainder of her days in prosperous health.

Jesus asked His disciples, **"Who touched me?"** This woman's faith was so intense, Jesus felt virtue leave His body the second she placed her hand on His garment. The disciples wondered how Jesus could ask such a question. Couldn't He see there were hundreds of people crushing in around them? Naturally, Jesus was aware of the volume of people, but there was only one distinguishing force behind one person's faith that had touched Him. The woman realizing that by touching His clothing her body was instantly healed, became frightened. Nervously she confessed. *"It was I."* Jesus turned looking upon her with compassion filled eyes. **"Daughter, your faith (your confidence and trust in Me) has made you well! Go (enter) into peace (untroubled, undisturbed, well-being)."**

She not only was healed in her spirit, soul, and body, but she was freed in her mind. The determined faith of this woman is an example for all of us. She finally made up her mind to stop listening to the voices of others trying to convince her the life she had was as good as it was going to get. Needless to say, this woman's perseverance developed out of a heart empowered by faith. Her faith proved Jesus could do the impossible! The desire of her heart was fueled by an insatiable faith which produced divine results. Had she kept listening to the opinions of others, and remained a hostage of her mind feeling sorry for herself, look what she would've missed! Every female reading this book has the option to choose spiritual freedom. You don't have to settle for an unproductive life. Women today are no different from the woman with the issue of blood. Oh, we new millennium dolls may know a thing or two about a thing or two. Yet we don't know God says prosperous living belongs to us. This woman received her healing! She sought after prosperity relentlessly! Need I say more?

However, this is a decision we must make for ourselves. If we want to see progressive, positive changes in our lives, we're going to have to get off the couch. Just as Jesus was there for the woman with the issue of blood over 2000 years ago, He's available to women today! Jesus has given every female permission to cast all of her cares (issues) on Him. Not some of them. All of them. (I Pet. 5:7) Girlfriend, all means all! We don't have to live in bondage. Many times the enemy deceives us with smoke and mirrors. He camouflages ugly self-afflicting issues that continuously create emotional problems for us. The next time a new issue crops up, run! Crawl if you have to! But take it straight to Jesus! Stretch forth your hand! Believe with all of your heart. Then boldly declare with faith. "I believe!"

One of the promises from God is we can have all things, including deliverance from nagging, often destructive issues. The enemy is going to purposely come against us to shake our faith. Don't be fooled! He's a clever devil always at work, if doing nothing more than generating a lot of emotional upheaval in our lives. Where do you think low self-esteem comes from? It's an emotion meant to entrap us. The enemy wants to stop us from discovering everything God has equipped within us to pursue passions for prosperity. Why? Because if we don't possess self-confidence, we won't make any attempt to start something. We'll be convinced we can't, or won't finish. This is also another form of procrastination.

To get pass procrastination we must read God's Word everyday. Meditate on His Word day and night. We're going to have to develop courage. Faith requires speaking a vision and/or dream as though it already exists. (Rom. 4:17) That means we're going to need a new vocabulary, which can only come by reading God's Word. Even if we read for fifteen minutes a day, it's a start. I suggest reading the Word aloud. Our ears will hear what we're saying, which will help strengthen our heart, spirit, soul, and mind. This also increases our level of belief. Girlfriend, putting off today for tomorrow is not wise. Today is what we have right now. Take advantage of it. Procrastination is our enemy!

One of the ways I overcame the mindset of always putting things off was to sit down and make myself a list of priorities. For me it was essential that I physically saw what was most important to set my faith in motion. I divided my list into two columns.

Go Beyond Your Dreams
(Live Them!)

One column was for my household responsibilities: cleaning, laundry, cooking, grocery shopping, etc. I broke them down into days and times. The second column was for my private times: praying, reading the Bible, writing, reading books by other authors, phone calls, etc. I did the same thing with column two. Once I established how much time would be given to each list, I was able to better focus on doing those things. I also wrote a short commitment to myself. *I will not put any (natural) thing before God.* I made a copy for my bathroom, refrigerator and bedroom closet door where I could see my commitment everyday.

Girlfriend, I won't pretend it was easy stepping out of my comfort zone. I preferred to only write on weekends. But I'll admit, very little writing was getting done. I did almost anything to keep from sitting down at my computer. I told myself I had every right to do absolutely nothing on the weekend after working all week. I had every right to sleep as late as I wanted, or not get dressed if I didn't want. There were plenty of times when I'd come home from work, sit down on the couch, watch TV, and go to bed without so much as a thought about writing.

After compiling this priority list, I realized what was more important. It didn't take me long to adjust my thinking. For a brief period I declined social invitations. I began taking advantage of Friday nights by writing. I did laundry while I was on the computer. I still do laundry on Fridays. Since I worked eight hours a day, five days a week, I'd cook enough food on Sundays to nuke left-overs in the microwave. If I had to grocery shop, I got up early on Saturday morning. This freed me up for the remainder of the day to research on the internet and write. Now that I'm divorced, my home stays clean longer, so housekeeping has been cut in half. I take advantage of reading during my commute on the bus to work. As I previously mentioned, I'm not a morning person so I pray and/or read God's Word each night before I go to bed.

Let me encourage you to write down a list of everything you do for realigning your time management. This list will be a visual reminder to overcome procrastination. It will help you see how much time you waste throughout the course of your day. If you can see what most of your time is spent on, you'll realize you don't have as much 'free' time as you thought you did. The idea of writing down what you do everyday becomes a blue print, separating what's important from what is less important. It will also highlight areas where you're likely to slip back into procrastinating again. In between carrying out these priorities, listen to Word tapes. They can help keep you motivated. Listen to music that will minister to your spirit instead of reaching for the remote turning the TV on. The more you begin maximizing your time, the less time you'll find yourself making excuses for putting things off.

Go Beyond Your Dreams
(Live Them!)

Now, I know this isn't going to be what you may want to hear, but it's only fair that I tell you, your friends might have to take a back seat for a little while. At least until procrastination no longer controls you. Common sense tells us there are going to be people who will not want changes taking place in your life—especially goal-oriented changes. Whether we like it, or not, striving toward goals for betterment often leads to intimidation for others. Girlfriend, there isn't anything you can do about that. Regrettably, the enemy uses the people who are closest to us. So don't be offended when a family member or a dear friend says, *"what makes you think you can do something like that? It'll never happen!"*

One of the smartest things you can do for yourself is spiritually prepare for opposition. You can best believe negative comments are sure to come your way. Girlfriend, prepare yourself. You are going to get your feelings hurt! Not everybody is going to take kindly to this new attitude of yours. But silently remind yourself. *"Who are these people to speak against my prosperity?"* That question alone should put things back into perspective. The moment you make the decision to stop delaying your dreams, there won't be anyone, or anything that'll be able to prevent you from bringing forth the vision. Sadly, people seldom want others to recognize there are greater potentials on the inside of them. The longer you continue to put your dreams on the back burner, the better they feel. But who are *they*?

Girlfriend, the only person who can stop you from achieving the desires of your heart, is you! Jesus said you can have whatsoever you pray, according to the size of your faith. Even if you start with small faith, nurture it until it grows into big faith. Manifestation largely depends on how strongly you believe that faith is capable of bringing what you desire. Don't be swayed by what you see (through natural eyes), or what you hear from others who doubt you'll ever do anything more than what you're doing right now. Constantly energize your mind by reading over your list of priorities to remind yourself why you're doing this. And, whatever you do. Don't go back to sitting on the couch eating potato chips and watching TV when you could be working toward establishing prosperity!

In the book of Habakkuk, we're encouraged, that while the vision may tarry, we're to wait on it! Girlfriend, don't give up on you, or your dreams! (Hab. 2:3) Our God is not a father who gives broken promises. He can't lie! If God said He'll do it, you can best believe (with all of your heart), that He's going to do it! (Num. 23:19) It's going to take the God-kind of spiritual and mental strength to hold onto your faith. So woman beware! Once the enemy takes notice of how serious you are about having what you desire, buckle up your platform shoes for battle! He's going to do everything he can (and will use anybody), to try to persuade you from sitting down to write your vision. The enemy strategically plays tricks with our minds. He likes twisting our thoughts to create doubt. *"What's writing anything down going to prove? Why bother?"* It's crazy questions like those that will come out of nowhere! Girlfriend, if he can get you to doubt the Word of God, half of the devil's work is done. But the devil is a liar! Jesus said it, and I believe it! Stop the devil right in his tracks. Show him whose boss!

When you have negative thoughts, declare what the Word of God says and get to writing down that vision! The enemy is afraid of what you're capable of doing. You should not be afraid of anything he might try to use against you. God's got your back! The enemy doesn't have any power over you, especially when it comes to the welfare of the children of God. Remember, faith must be established in the heart. It serves little, or no purpose neatly tucked away in our heads. That's why God instructs us to write the vision down and make it plain. (Hab. 2:2) Be specific with exactly how you see it. God wants you to see His vision for you through spiritual eyes. And once that happens, there's no turning back! That's what the devil knows. He knows if you begin seeing yourself in the vision, he's in trouble. Girlfriend, in spite of any hardships you might experience, you mustn't lose heart! Remain firmly planted in God's Word, trusting Him all the way! (Isa. 40:8) Constantly read over your vision. And, whatever you do, don't feed into how someone else thinks or feels about your dream. God gave it to you. Not them! I'm thoroughly convinced God-given visions and dreams aren't expected to be understood by anyone else except the woman to whom it has been given.

Do you know the story in the Bible about Noah? His family thought he was nuts! It wasn't easy for Noah to persuade them about his vision for building the ark. But Noah believed what God told him. He chose to let those doubting people say, think and feel whatever they wanted. Noah held onto the Word of God.

I challenge you to remind yourself of these words when moments of verbal negativity flair up against you. "Who are *'they'* to speak against my dreams and desires?" As a faith precaution, be mindful not to allow yourself to get caught up in people's bondage (focusing more on the thoughts/actions of others). If you're not spiritually perceptive to the motives behind certain words, you may start to care more about what *they* say, rather than embrace what God says. Talk about your vision as if it already exists. (Isa. 55:11) Faith should always be thought of as taking place now. Keep the vision before your eyes, and God's Word in your mouth.

John 15:7 reads:

> **If you live in Me [abide vitally united to Me] and My words remain in you *and* continue to live in your hearts,**

Go Beyond Your Dreams
(Live Them!)

ask whatever you will, and it shall be done for you. (AMP)

Most women think hope is the same thing as having faith. They're not entirely right. They're not entirely wrong. God speaks of having hope throughout the Bible, so that tells me it's a good thing to have hope, but it's so much better when you have faith. Unlike hope, faith sees positive changes taking place in your life for the better. Faith becomes an attitude. Faith stimulates the heart for believing in the impossible. Faith is a well made up mind. Faith is not allowing someone to talk you out of what you desire. Faith isn't a feeling, nor is it an emotion. Faith is action. Faith overrides hope. True faith is when we believe with all of our heart the impossible is possible! Faith planted (deeply rooted) inside the heart begins to open doors that no man can shut. Faith is knowing that God will direct your steps to be in the right place at the right time. Faith is believing God will bring people across your path to help usher in your dreams. I cannot stress enough. Women need to possess a heart of faith for everything. You must believe God is able to do whatever you ask of Him.

While you may experience attacks of weakness (because you will), ask God to give you emotional strength to defeat those feelings of weariness. Faith is a gift from God that is freely extended to you. Why wouldn't you want to take advantage of it to accomplish your dreams? Nothing is ever quite as simple as we'd like to think. Therefore, don't assume making dreams come true is easy to achieve. It's going to take lots of perseverance to bring dreams to pass. But you can do this!

Girlfriend, don't be afraid to put faith into action! God pre-destined your life for success long before you were even conceived. As your creator, God knew what His plans were for you, and your future.

Jeremiah 1:5 reads:

> **Before I formed you in the womb I knew [and] approved of you [as My chosen instrument], and before you were born I separated *and* set you apart, consecrating you; [and] I appointed you as a prophet to the nations.** (AMP)

I've learned through the teachings of my pastor there is a key element required to spring faith into action. It's quite simple. **SAY IT!** We should continuously say (confess) what it is we desire to see come to pass. I've also been taught there are actually two kinds of faith: (1) The heart of faith which produces results, and (2) The mind of faith that will probably have you waiting, waiting, waiting, and still waiting. Let me give you an illustration of a woman with unwavering faith, who finally received what she believed. This woman, who I'll call Diane, is in need of reliable transportation. The car she's currently driving won't last much longer, but she refuses to pay another dime for repairs. Diane desires to own a particular car, but the starting price is over $30,000. When Diane prayed, she believed God would answer that need. Diane believed she'd receive the financial means to afford to buy that car. So instead of doing nothing, Diane sprang into action. She began showing God how much faith she had in His Word by going to a dealership to test drive her dream car. Diane cut out a picture of the car from a magazine advertisement. She taped the picture on her refrigerator where she could gaze at it everyday. Diane repeatedly confessed driving the car in her favorite color, and the exact model she wanted. She never doubted all things were possible with God. Diane wouldn't allow herself to be influenced by others. Despite what family members were saying, she trusted her heart (not her mind), that it was only a matter of time before she'd be taking those same family members for a ride in her new car.

Well, two months passed. Diane still didn't have enough money saved for a down payment. And, if that wasn't enough, her old clunker needed another $600.00 in repairs. Still, she stood firm believing that God was able. Diane was determined not to doubt Him, or His Word. Every time she looked upon the picture taped on the refrigerator, Diane thanked and praised God for answered prayers.

One afternoon four weeks later while Diane was at work, the salesman from the dealership phoned. The exact make, model and color of the car she wanted had been delivered to their lot earlier that morning. Instantly, Diane saw herself behind the wheel! Without thinking she uttered, "God, I want that car!" The salesman (he didn't hear her), began explaining the purchasing terms. The car could be hers without a down payment. The salesman's manager was willing to accept her old car as a trade-in for $500.00 more than what they had previously discussed. And, to sweeten the deal, after running a credit check, Diane qualified for a low interest rate. The salesman asked, "when do you want to come in to get your car?" There wasn't any doubt in Diane's mind. God had opened a door to purchase her dream car. "I can come in after work!" Diane confidently answered. She believed she had received the results of her faith. By putting faith into action, Diane went to test drive a car with no idea how she'd ever afford to actually buy it. By trusting God at His Word, Diane's dreams came true! She never wavered in her faith.

Now, it wouldn't be fair if I didn't give you an example of faith that operates in the head. We have another woman I'll call Betty. She's been living in a cramped apartment much longer than she originally thought she would. Lately, Betty has been desiring to buy a house. Following weeks of consistent prayer God began orchestrating a scenario for Betty to move forward by faith.

Go Beyond Your Dreams
(Live Them!)

It was on a Sunday afternoon following church service when a reliable friend told Betty that she'd recently purchased her first home. Betty found herself getting excited. She started thinking if her friend could buy a house, so could she. Betty's friend readily explained the house she bought was located in an area where new houses were being built everyday. The friend informed Betty that mortgage rates were currently at an advantage for first time home buyers. Then the friend shared how she prayed in faith and found scriptures in the Bible to read everyday, which reinforced her faith.

After the two women parted, the idea of owning a house appealed to Betty even more. She believed God could do the same for her. Betty instantly hoped God would give her the desires of her heart. Unfortunately, as Betty reached her car in the church parking lot, she began questioning if faith could really work for her. With all the information Betty's friend passed on within those few minutes, Betty drove past the neighborhood convenience store. Instead of taking a couple of minutes to run inside to buy a newspaper, she failed to see an opportunity. Betty didn't understand by not stopping she had done nothing to put her faith into action. The newspaper was an opportunity to search the real estate section for homes that were listed for sale. Betty's friend was thoughtful enough to supply her with a business card of the realtor she used. She also gave Betty the bank manager's name who helped secure her mortgage.

When Betty got home she took the information and tossed it inside one of the kitchen drawers. Betty deceived herself by thinking she had as much faith as anyone else. Sadly, she didn't fully understand prayers alone weren't enough to move God closer to blessing her with a dream home.

Unbeknownst to Betty, she had unwittingly elected to keep faith in her head. Over the following weeks Betty continued doing nothing to build faith within her heart. Betty's mind swayed her to believe God already knew how much she wanted to move out of her apartment. In her mind, Betty didn't think she had to do anything, except wait for God to bless her. It was that kind of thinking that led her to sit down in front of the TV day after day. Faith without any action to back it up was only faith in Betty's head. She couldn't foresee she was going to remain an apartment renter for a while longer. What's even sadder, Betty neglected to reprogram her mindset by reading God's Word to gain insight for increasing her faith. Had she taken the time to read her Bible for a greater understanding, Betty would've understood she'd only been hoping to move into a new house. She would've realized her desire was very possible with God.

Betty isn't the only woman who believes faith is released through the mind. It may start there, but faith must channel its way from the head down to the heart where it can be nourished by the Word of God. Then you *have* to do something! The bottom line is this. Girlfriend, you can have all the faith you want inside your heart, but until it moves your heart, and you put it into action, nothings going to happen! Action! Action! Action! Faith is fueled by action!

Not once will I tell you possessing faith is going to be easy. It's not. However, should you find yourself becoming somewhat frustrated (cause you're human), don't grow weary! You're stronger than you might think! Don't faint! If the manifestation is taking longer than you expected, believe (in your heart), it will come to pass! Delayed doesn't mean denied. It simply means God is still putting everything into its proper place.

Whether you can physically see doors opening or not, have faith in your vision. God is still in control! He'll open doors of opportunity for you in *His timing.* Truth be told, usually we're not as ready to receive what we pray for as much as we'd like to think we are. Quite often we're still in need of maturing both spiritually and mentally. Sometimes it's a matter of God correcting a few unproductive attitudes and emotions that will hinder the longevity of our prosperity. Whatever the case may be, God knows precisely when it is the appropriate time to give you the rewards of your faith. God is all-knowing (Omniscient), which means the fruition of your faith will arrive on schedule. The manifestation will arrive at the moment God pre-destined for you. So relax! We can't walk around in doubt or be dismayed by what we perceive to not be happening.

God wants us to trust Him completely. (Isa. 41:10) He's so awesome! God has knowledge of what we need even before we ask.

Matthew 6:8 reads:

> **Do not be like them, for your Father knows what you need before you ask Him.** (AMP)

All things are available to us. Our Father will supply every one of our needs! But it's imperative that we believe God is able. You should also bear in mind God is a God of exchange. Many women probably will not agree with this, but if you stop for a moment to think about what I'm about to say, it might register in a different light. Having the mindset of always wanting to get something for nothing speaks volumes about a person's character. You didn't hear me say selfish. I didn't say it! The fact is, you probably will have to give up something, but it will only be for a short while. Anything worth having usually involves sacrifice. When you're finally living out your dreams, those sacrifices would've been all well worth it. You'll look back and wonder what all the fuss was about.

The spiritual aerobic exercises I developed were a tremendous help in my pursuit of establishing the kind of faith that I believed would bring results. I shared this with you because working through daily spiritual aerobics allows you to see yourself in the vision. The more you pump up your faith, the more it

Go Beyond Your Dreams
(Live Them!)

increases your level of belief. As you get into a habit of exercising steps 1, 2, and 3, something starts to take place within you.

You'll know without any doubt your dreams have every chance of coming true. (II Cor. 5:7) Now granted, strong faith may appear to be a bit over-the-top for others. But it's going to look even crazier when those same negative people cannot close their mouths from watching your dream unfold right before their very eyes! Girlfriend, don't ever be embarrassed for holding tight with both hands (feet too, if need be), for what you believe is possible with God! You'll probably get tired of me reminding you of this, but possession of heart filled faith won't be easy. There'll be times when you're going to come up against dumb stuff. It's only intended to get you off your mark. Stand firm! Don't move!

A daily reading of God's Word is a great regimen for stability, which is why it's included in my spiritual aerobic exercises. God's Word provides spiritual strength, especially when we feel like we won't make it through another day. Prosperity will not come without a fight. These exercises are meant to bring positive change into your life spiritually, mentally, physically and financially. If your spirit is at peace, your mind will be clear. If you no longer procrastinate, you'll have the zeal required to pursue your dreams. Nothing, and no one will be able to stop you!

One of my favorite men in the Bible is Abraham. Now that man had faith! Abraham was going to offer his son Isaac as a sacrifice unto the Lord because he trusted God at His Word. There's a great deal to be learned from him. Here's a little nugget about Abraham's faith. In the book of **Romans 4:20-21 it reads:**

> **No unbelief *or* distrust made him waver (doubtingly question) concerning the promise of God, but he grew strong *and* was empowered by faith as he gave praise *and* glory to God, Fully satisfied *and* assured that God was able *and* mighty to keep His word *and* to do what He had promised. (AMP)**

Alright girlfriend, get up off the couch. Complete your list of priorities, and start writing down your vision. It's time to put your faith to work! Keep dreaming, and dream as big as your heart will allow you to dream! You can do this! You can have whatsoever your heart desires! Don't be afraid to step out on faith! Don't be afraid to trust God at His Word! Both faith and the unfailing Word of God will sustain you, even when it looks like the impossible isn't going to materialize into the possible. Jesus said with God *all* things are possible to those who believe.

You will only disappoint yourself if you don't follow through on the visions and dreams God has implanted inside of your heart. He put them there for

Go Beyond Your Dreams
(Live Them!)

you and I to lead lives filled with peace, joy and abundantly satisfied while we're in the earth. The riches of Heaven await us, but for now, while we're down here on planet earth, God wants us to have the riches He's provided for us now. Unless we fail to tap into the many gifts and talents that all of us possess, and then we miss the opportunities of a lifetime, living paycheck-to-paycheck, wandering aimlessly wondering what could have been. Well, wonder no more. You owe it to yourself to be everything and all things that God has created you to be!

Go Beyond Your Dreams
(Live Them!)

CHAPTER 3
YOU ARE BLESSED

And God Blessed them and said to them. Be fruitful, multiply, and fill the earth, and subdue it [using all its vast resources in the service of God and man]; and have dominion over the fish of the sea, the birds of the air, and over every living creature that moves upon the earth. (AMP)

Genesis 1:28

Our Heavenly Father is the most loving, the most compassionate, the most generous father you or I will ever have. Unquestionably, biological fathers love their daughters too. Most daddies will do whatever is necessary to see that their daughter is happy. On the other hand, God has the kind of love that goes deeper than any love we could ever humanly imagine. From the moment we accept Jesus Christ into our hearts, we're adopted into a royal kingdom. Within a blink of an eye, we go from being cursed by sin, to being blessed by the forgiveness of our sins. God promises to bless His children in such a way, we couldn't receive it all!

Galatians 3:8-9 reads:

And the Scripture, foreseeing that God would justify (declare righteous, put in

right standing with Himself) the Gentiles in consequence of faith, proclaimed the Gospel [foretelling the glad tidings of a Savior long beforehand] to Abraham in the promise, saying, In you shall all the nations [of the earth] be blessed. So then, those who are people of faith are blessed *and* made happy *and* favored by God [as partners in fellowship] with the believing *and* trusting Abraham. (AMP)

Striving to lead diligent and disciplined lifestyles are beneficial faith building structures. Girlfriend, you do yourself a disservice when you utter things like, "I can't afford that." Get out of the habit of saying, "I can do without buying that." I don't care if there's only one dollar in your wallet, think rich! Tell yourself that through faith, you will be able to afford whatsoever your heart desires! Speak into your life! God is the wealthiest man you'll ever know! He's abundant in spirit, power, truth, and financially wealthy!

Let me briefly take a minute to share something with you. Once I finally got it through my thick skull to reframe from sprouting the opposite of what God's Word says about my finances, the small amount of money I had left over from payday actually began stretching further in between pay checks. It was imperative that my money start increasing almost immediately. Hubby was gone! I was left on my own to pay a lot of household expenses, including a sizable mortgage. And, if you own a house, you know banks don't play when it comes to mortgage payments!

Well, getting back to my pay check, I cannot explain it. I'm not even going to try. The only explanation I can offer for the dramatic turn around in my finances is this. I'm a good steward (pay tithes- 10% of my earnings). I'm a giver. That's not boasting. I'm glorifying God for what He's done for me financially. You want to hear how good God is? Ten years ago when I relocated back home, God opened a door (within a week), for an opportunity to work at a law firm. It began as a temporary position, with temp wages. But did I care, so long as I could eat? Anyway, I watched God move on my behalf. Within two months of working at the firm I was hired full time. This meant medical benefits, paid sick days, and paid vacation days. Ten years later I've received raises for every year that I've been with the firm. I've gone from one week of vacation to four weeks. God blessed me with a great job. So I know firsthand that He truly wants us to live and enjoy our lives. God has a compassionate love for His children. He desires to shower us with good things—His absolute best. In the book of Psalms there's a verse of scripture that literally jumped off the page while I was researching for this book. I hope as I pass it on to you, it will bless you as much as it blessed me.

Psalms 34:10 reads:

The young lions lack food and suffer hunger, but they who seek (inquire of and require) the Lord [by right of their need and on the authority of His Word], none of them shall lack any beneficial thing. (AMP)

Wow! That's good news! Girlfriend, don't profess to be blessed, but deep down on the inside not believe that blessings are yours to receive. That's being double-minded. You hinder your prayers going back and forth with faith. Have you ever stopped to consider where ideas, visions, and dreams originate? God generously implants them inside our hearts long before we're conceived in the womb. He already knows exactly which direction our lives are going because He is our Alpha (the beginning). He is our Omega (the end). What we choose to do in the middle depends on us. God has given everyone of us free will. He's a gentleman. God won't show up where He's not welcomed. However, by making Him our number one priority for direction over our lives, our thoughts, emotions and actions (living in right standing), we have the promise of receiving the desires of our heart. A full commitment to God's ways is assurance dreams will come to pass. (Ps. 37:4-5) God asks that we delight ourselves in Him, and He will give us desires impressed upon the requests of our hearts. We first must commit ourselves unto Him, trusting in His Word.

Go Beyond Your Dreams
(Live Them!)

The promises of God are *yes* and *amen*. How hard is that to understand? "Yes." I'll do it God's way. "Amen." I believe He's already done it. There isn't anything complicated about that. God won't watch dreams go unfulfilled when He looks upon a sincere heart standing in faith. Every heart that trusts Him and desires His heart for their lives to fulfill their dreams, will receive. A woman who is determined, steadfast and working her faith to its fullest potential does not go unrecognized by God. He honors her diligence to believe He is able, no matter what.

Girlfriend, just because you're still waiting for something to look like it's changing, or nothing appears to be happening as quickly as you thought it would, doesn't mean you've been looked over. Having to wait on manifestation is not any implication you've been forgotten by God. Renew your mind so you can keep a sharp look out for the schemes of the enemy. He'll try to trick you by planting thoughts of denial inside your head. Shake yourself. Hold fast to your confessions. Believe that you've already received the reality of your faith!

You are the daughter of the Almighty God! That's worth jumping to your feet and giving Him praise! (Acts 3:8) The same awesome God who raised Jesus from the tomb, is the same God who is able to raise you above others to show Himself strong in your life. Continue to dream! Can you think of anyone else more deserving of having her God-given dreams come true other than yourself? God gave His vision to you with your name engraved on it. It's God's will that you live successfully in every area of your life. Stop listening to people who want to fill your head with doubt. You're a blessed woman! You can have whatsoever you believe is possible! If no one else believes that you're capable of going all the way by faith, you believe in you! Never mind them! Let me share this scripture for times like that.

I Peter 2:15 reads:

> **For it is God's will *and* intention that by doing right [your good and honest lives] should silence (muzzle, gag) the ignorant charges *and* ill-informed criticisms of foolish persons. (AMP)**

Need I say more? I encourage you to strut with your head held high, putting one foot in front of the other, walking boldly toward your destiny. Dress your blessed self in royalty, accessorizing with dignity and pride. Girlfriend, when I get dressed in the morning for work, I leave the house looking like I'm an attorney! My God told me to be confident in whom He says I am! I dress the part of a blessed successful and prosperous woman! (Heb. 10:35) The way a woman looks and feels sends a boost to her spirit. A self-inspired feeling of personal awareness stimulates the mind. However, it's okay when you have a bad hair day. Don't beat yourself up. You're human. What female hasn't encountered a groggy

Go Beyond Your Dreams
(Live Them!)

moment? Like any father will do, whenever God sees His daughters upset, He wraps His loving arms about us. He comforts us in the safe, secure and assurance of His love. God reminds us in spite of our emotions, we're still His baby girls. God understands our times of weakness better than anyone. He loves us no less because of them. When you've done everything you know to do in the natural, continue acting in faith. That weary feeling will pass. Your dream is going to happen! But you must prove yourself worthy of the dream by keeping God's Word close to your heart.

In the Book of Exodus, God told Moses he was the chosen one to bring the Israelites out of Egypt from under the terrible rule of Pharaoh. God *had* to keep the promise which He swore to Abraham, Isaac, and Jacob to bring His chosen people into a land flowing with milk and honey. I'm going to skip ahead. You'll have to read Exodus for yourself. God didn't exactly make an act of faith smooth sailing for Moses. He was tested over and over again. Faith isn't about rubbing a genie's lamp. You work for it. God wants to know He can trust us with the vision. When we accept our pre-destined assignments, He expects us to pass tests. And, if you pass them with flying colors, the rewards of God will blow your mind!

But let me get back to the story about God's chosen ones. The Israelites were finally freed after enduring over 400 years in slavery. God did such a whammy on Pharaoh, that He released the Israelites with the riches of Egypt! Whatever the Israelites could load onto carts and the backs of their oxen, they took with them. The Israelites walked through the gates of Egypt singing, and praising God. As they left the captivity of Egypt behind, the favor of God was upon them.

Unfortunately, many of the Israelites still suffered from poverty mindsets. While journeying through the desert under the guidance of Moses, they began longing for Egypt. In their fearful, doubting minds they at least understood their place in Egypt. The unknown petrified them, even though God had given them the promise for a better future. The Israelites couldn't see (the vision) God had a purposeful plan over their lives. There are women much like that today. It was a poor self image which kept the Israelites inflicted by fear. They had no concept that faith wasn't believing what they could see. Faith was believing God at His Word, long before they saw anything. The Israelites traveled through the desert under the heavy influences of Pharaoh's bondage and deception. They had convinced themselves the harsh conditions enforced by Pharaoh were better than anything God might have for them. Sadly, the Israelites roamed the desert following years of having been stripped of their godly identities. Identity theft isn't anything new. The enemy has stolen identities ever since he fell from Heaven. The only difference is now he has a lot of cohorts to assist him.

Go Beyond Your Dreams
(Live Them!)

Instead of trusting God's Word, the Israelites murmured and complained to Moses about God. That was not a smart thing. For forty years they walked the desert going around in circles. It wasn't until those faithless generations died in the wilderness when God began moving forward the remnant of people to the Promised Land who had remained faithful.

God instructed Moses to tell the next generation (the Joshua generation), that if they would obey His voice, and keep His covenant, they'd be a peculiar treasure unto Him above all people. (Ex. 19:5) God also told the Israelites that if they followed the instruction of His Word, everything they did would bring them prosperity. Does that sound familiar? God still expects the same from us today. He commands reverence and obedience from His children.

Deuteronomy 29:9 reads:

Therefore keep the words of this covenant and do them, that you may deal wisely *and* prosper in all that you do. (AMP)

The old Israelites were frightened people. It didn't matter how many times they witnessed the mighty hand of God perform miracle after miracle on their behalf, they still found something to complain about. They even had the audacity to accuse Moses of leading them out of Egypt just so they could die in the wilderness. (Ex. 15:24; 16:3; 17:3)

The Israelites had a God-appointed opportunity to live out the remainder of their years in a land flowing with milk and honey (the Promised Land), but they couldn't see it. The enemy had purposely hidden God's vision from them.

Have you ever heard that old saying, as much as things change, they stay the same? Quite often mindsets go unchanged even when it involves the things of God. There are saints who to this day, *still* find it hard to believe God's Word will part a Red Sea for them. They don't completely trust Him. They trust God a little bit, and trust man more. These are usually the same people constantly whining and complaining before God. Let me clarify something, if I may. There's a big misconception the promises God spoke to men and women in the Bible over two thousand years ago don't apply to us today. That has got to be one of the biggest deceptions spread by the enemy. We serve the same God who created the earth, the sun, the moon, the planets, the stars, and Heaven. He's the same God who created Adam and Eve. God doesn't change. Every promise He made to Abraham are available to all saints today. God's Word will never change! He's the same yesterday, today, tomorrow, and forever! The promise of a land flowing with milk and honey even exists in the new millennium. It's a different type of Canaan land God desires for mankind today. But nonetheless, He wants to give us the same thing; a life flowing in abundance.

Go Beyond Your Dreams
(Live Them!)

Psalms 105:8-11 reads:

> **He is [earnestly] mindful of His covenant *and* forever it is imprinted on His heart, the word which He commanded *and* established to a thousand generations, The covenant which He made with Abraham, and His sworn promise to Isaac, Which He confirmed to Jacob as a statute, to Israel as an everlasting covenant, Saying Unto you will I give the land of Canaan as your measured portion, possession, *and* inheritance. (AMP)**

God hasn't forgotten not one of the promises He made to Abraham. Just because we're the generation of fast cars, cell phones, IPods, computers, flat screen TV's, and more new fangled technology than we know what to do with, the same God who spoke to Moses on Mount Sinai, is the same God speaking to us today. As a seed of Abraham, the promises (inheritance) of God belong to us!

Acts 3:25 reads:

> **You are the descendants (sons) of the prophets and the heirs of the covenant which God made *and* gave to your forefathers, saying to Abraham, And in your Seed (Heir) shall all the families of the earth be blessed *and* benefited. (AMP)**

Girlfriend, you are a blessed woman of God! Take action by stopping every scheme, strategy, lie and false accusation the enemy throws your way! It is God's will and purpose for you to have prosperity and success in every area of your life. However, it's equally important for us to understand it's His will that we develop an intimate relationship with Him. God wants to be included in our daily lives. God takes pleasure in the prosperity of His people. (III Jn. 2) Women who are empowered in their spirit will always succeed in the things of God. With heart filled faith, we can be assured through our acts of obedience, the blessing (manifestation), is made available in the spirit realm the moment we open our mouths in prayer. Dreams become realities the second we open our hearts in faith. Digesting faith into our hearts through God's Word creates a connection between the natural realm and the spirit realm. Faith starts preparing your words to bring those things which you are speaking into the natural realm. We *must* say what we want to see!

Matthew 21:22 reads:

> **Absolutely everything, ranging from small to large, as you make it a part of your believing prayer, gets included as you lay hold of God. (THE MESSAGE)**

One of the things I sometimes struggle with is lending a compassionate ear to one of my friends when she's in need of financial assistance. Listening is all well and fine, but having nothing tangible to offer is a bummer! I can't tell you how upsetting it is not to be able to do anything more than just listen. It hurts that I can't be of more help. And, you want to know something else? I don't like it, especially when the need is grave! That's why more and more it has become increasingly clear to me that I want to be in a position of financial overflow. I know I'm blessed, but I want to go to another dimension. One of my many dreams is to be blessed (financially) to be a blessing to others. While I also desire to be a successful author, my motives are not selfish. Girlfriend, unless we possess wealth, how can we possibly contribute to the needs of others? We can't!

The Word of God tells me to believe I'm blessed, so I do. Regardless what my present situation may look like, I believe when I pray a petition before God, He hears every word. To encourage myself I chant around my home, *"I'm the blessed seed of Abraham!"* Because let's face it. When the light bill is due, the car note is due and the money is funny, I don't exactly feel like royalty. So, who better to encourage me, than me? Maybe you should try singing or chanting the next time the enemy whispers in your ear that you're nothing, and never will be nothing. I'm telling you praise works! Take fifteen minutes, or however long necessary to reprogram your mind. Remember, faith doesn't come without action.

Let me ask you something. Have you ever experienced a situation where you needed someone to not only listen to your plight, you needed them to help you out? Maybe (like me), you were too embarrassed to ask for help. Then, to your surprise that same person blessed you beyond the need! That's the favor of God! He promised to supply our every need.

Philippians 4:19 reads:

You can be sure that God will take care of everything you need, his generosity exceeding even yours in the glory that pours from Jesus. (THE MESSAGE)

Have you ever had strangers bend over backwards to help you, and they wouldn't stop until your need had been satisfied? Usually the person doesn't have a clue why he or she feels compelled to help you. That's God! He's even able to cause our enemies to respond in our favor. Mankind might use manipulation to get a need met, but thank God, we don't have to resort to those measures! (Prov. 16:7) (Jer. 15:11) Familiarizing yourself with God's Word concerning His favor and mercy erases feelings of uncertainty. That's why it's imperative to consistently do reading aerobic exercises to keep our hearts filled with faith, and our minds renewed in who God says we are.

Go Beyond Your Dreams
(Live Them!)

There's a common mistake most women make. I've done it myself. We allow others to tell us there is something wrong about expecting favors. Girlfriend, how else is God going to supply our every need, except through another human being? God (and only God) has the power to change the minds and hearts of people who normally wouldn't lift a finger to help us. When it comes to the welfare of God's children, He'll move mountains for them! God is like that! So don't let the enemy use somebody to get in your face with a motive to talk you out of a blessing! As your faith increases, the enemy will use whoever he can to attack you. Therefore, learn to keep your spiritual skills sharpened. When opportunities present themselves you're going to need to recognize (discern) it's a favor from God and not a glossed over distraction (a counterfeit blessing).

This is probably a good time as any to add another exercise to step 3. I kinda slipped that one in on you. But isn't that what aerobic instructors do in those classes? You're sweating, working out as hard as you can to keep up with the rest of the class, and just when you think, I've got it now—bam!

I like using men and women from the Bible as examples. I'll use Pharaoh again. By the time God finished with him, Pharaoh's heart was crushed. In a moment of despair, he let the Israelites leave Egypt with all the silver and the gold! God's chosen people left with the spoils (wealth) of Egypt! The Israelites went from suffering horrendous treatment, to the glorious deliverance of God's mighty right hand! They had the favor of God resting up on them. Now, that's what I'm talking 'bout! God *used* Pharaoh to give His people everything they would need for their journey across the desert. Girlfriend start expecting favor from your Heavenly Father. As a blessed woman you should even begin to expect policies and rules to change in your favor. God's favor can supernaturally open doors of opportunities that were once off limits to you. His favor releases special treatment! But there is one more thing that I think will serve of importance to you. Please do not confuse favor for luck. They aren't the same thing. Luck is the world's way of thinking. Actually, luck is nothing more than a clever scheme by the enemy. If we say it was luck that made a particular situation turn out for our good, we eliminate God from the equation. People in general often refer to luck when good things happen for them. But as Christians, we should understand that luck doesn't have any place in our speech, or thought pattern. We're to give God the glory for every good thing that happens in our lives. We ought to know from where our blessings flow. So girlfriend, remove the word luck from your vocabulary. You're too blessed to depend on luck! You don't need it. God's got your back!

Proverbs 3:6 reads:

> **In all your ways know, recognize, *and* acknowledge Him, and He will direct**

Go Beyond Your Dreams (Live Them!)

and **make straight *and* plain your paths.** (AMP)

Who needs luck when we've got God on our side? Let man have his luck. I'd much rather have the favor of God! So girlfriend, start expecting the favor of God to show up on a daily basis for every area of your life. You are a blessed woman! In the next chapter I'll be talking about the things we say, and how we say them. Seldom do we realize the very words that proceed out of our mouths create the unproductive lifestyles in which we live. In order for faith to operate in our lives, we must develop an awareness of saying what God says in His Word about us.

Girlfriend, your ideas, visions, dreams, and desires deserve to come to fruition. Stop selling them short. Even more, stop selling yourself short. God has given you skills and abilities for a reason. It's very simple actually. God knew we would need two of His greatest components necessary for enriching our lives. The ability to have faith. The ability to speak things into existence. It's God's will to see all of His daughters leading whole, prosperous lives!

*Go Beyond Your Dreams
(Live Them!)*

***Go Beyond Your Dreams
(Live Them!)***

CHAPTER 4
DO NOT BE MOVED

As for me, in my prosperity I said, I shall never be moved.
God is in the midst of her, she shall not be moved; God will
help her right early [at the dawn of the morning] (AMP)

Psalms 30:6; 46:5

Are you conscientious of what you say, and how you say it? I can't tell you how many times I've blurted something out without thinking, immediately wishing I could take back my words. I have a question. Are you a woman who thinks of herself as having a positive out-look? That's good. Does most of what you say come out echoing on the heels of skepticism and negativity? That's not so good. Although the tongue is a small part of the body, it can do more damage than most people realize. I'll let you in on something. Regardless what you say, you will have whatsoever you say. Positive talk? You'll have what you say. Negative talk? You'll have what you say. (Jas. 3:5) Words that are released from our mouths take flight. They bring back what we've said. (Prov. 18:21) (Jer. 5:25)

A wise woman not only guards her heart, but she also governs her tongue. The heart and tongue go hand in hand. Our hearts trust in God's Word to do all things. Yet, we'll let our tongue talk our heart right out of believing God is able. Crazy, ugh? Girlfriend, please don't sabotage blessings by speaking foolishly. (Ps. 39:1) Say what God says. Bite your tongue if you must! Faith-filled words bring forth dreams!

Don't risk pushing your dream further away by mouthing negative words against what you are believing God to do on your behalf. Give thought to what you're saying and learn how to tame your tongue. Train yourself to think before speaking words contrary to God's Word.

James 3:8-9 reads:

> **But the human tongue can be tamed by no man. It is restless (undisciplined, irreconcilable) evil, full of deadly poison. With it we bless the Lord and Father, and with it we curse men who were made in God's likeness!** (AMP)

People have a way of saying things with very little regard for how their words affect the other party. I've been there, done that. There are also the ones who care less about the feelings of others, especially if the conversation expresses positive speech. More times than not, if you're carefully listening, their tone of voice serves as an indicator of their feelings towards you. I know you'll be itching

Go Beyond Your Dreams
(Live Them!)

to share (I can relate) this great vision God has given you, but proceed with caution.

There are two kinds of faith busters: (1) They don't hide how they feel about your wonderful news; and (2) They just outright resent you for having a dream. And, you know who *they* are. Faith buster number one shouldn't be a problem for you to spot right off the bat. Their facial expression and body language will reflect what's inside their heart. Faith buster number two is less likely to react. They show no expression. Their body language doesn't give any hint to what they're thinking. However, should you mention something else pertaining to your vision, and it immediately gets shot down, that's their way of letting you know how they really feel. Humor me for a minute. I want to use a hypothetical scenario using you in it. Okay, here goes.

You share intimate details with a friend. You explain that you're desiring to move into a larger house. Eye-balling you closely she responds, *"Why do you wanna buy another house? Isn't this house big enough for your husband, three kids, two dogs, cat, and bird? This is a nice house. Girl, houses are getting more expensive. How can you afford to buy a bigger house?"*

I know. You're surprised by your friend's reaction, aren't you? You thought she'd be jumping up-n-down happy for you, didn't you? Are you feeling slightly disappointed as her brown, scrutinizing eyes glare back at you? *"You're crazy to want to buy a bigger house. Didn't you tell me a couple of weeks ago your spending had gotten out of hand? What about your credit? What bank is gonna lend you money for a new mortgage? Honey, if I was you, I'd stay right where I am with a mortgage I know I can afford!"* she snickers.

First of all, you might not think you were asking for your girlfriend's opinion, but sure you were; the minute you opened your mouth. However, be that as it may, did you tell her you couldn't afford to buy a larger house? No! She assumed based on a previous conversation that you weren't financially stable. Instead of being happy for you, she started spewing negative reasons not to proceed with house hunting. Second of all, this is your vision! Not hers! While your friend's words were spilling over from a resentful heart, did you discern she said nothing to encourage you? Did you understand where her negative comments were actually coming from? Your faith busting friend was letting you know up front how she felt about your hearts desire. But can you think of anyone who deserves to live in a six bedroom house more than you and your family? Folks who don't have visions or dreams of their own, are more than happy to crush yours! (Ps. 10:3-5)

You may not want to hear this, but a decision to step out of your comfort zone is intimidating. Once you develop a well made up heart (faith) to possess a prospering lifestyle, it can shift to jealousy. Prepare yourself for faith busters, especially if those around you aren't dreamers. This illustration was meant to show you how challenges of your faith operate. It's a direct attempt by the enemy (using them), to try to discourage you from pursuing a vision that God has shown you is possible.

Psalms 109:2-3 reads:

> **For the mouths of the wicked and the mouth of deceit are opened against me; they have spoken to me and against me with lying tongues. They have compassed me about also with words of hatred and have fought against me without a cause.** (AMP)

You mustn't allow yourself to be sucked in (emotionally) by how someone else might feel about your vision. Like it, or not. Whether it's family or friends, everyone isn't going to agree with you, your faith, or your big dreams! After all, who are you to want to live in prosperity, especially when you come from a long line of poor relatives; a generational curse of poverty? Be not deceived! The enemy is going to place certain people at certain times on certain days in your way on purpose. It will be a deliberate plot to turn your mind against your heart by any means necessary. If you don't remember anything else you read in this book, remember this, a change of heart (doubting faith) will hinder your blessing(s). That's why I suggest doing spiritual aerobic exercises everyday. It's the only way God's Word will consistently be in your mouth, and on your tongue.

From one woman to another, may I suggest something else to you? Be absolutely certain the person you go to with your vision is trustworthy. Is this someone who will be in complete agreement with you? Do they believe all things are possible with God? Is this someone who will pray with you when you're feeling a moment of weakness? Can you rely on their support? Will they keep what's discussed private? Girlfriend, visions are close to God's heart. God-inspired visions and dreams are very special. Anyone (family, friends, co-workers, and church folk) who don't trust in the Word of God, or the limitless possibilities with God can block your blessing. You're probably better off not saying anything at all. This was a life lesson I had to learn.

Past experiences have taught me well. A few years back I spoke too soon when I shared my dream of becoming a published author. This person was quick to point out. *"Who do you think you are? You're no better than anybody else to think you can become a writer! You're gonna be working 9-to-5, five days a week just like the rest of us!"* Needless to say, after that I began keeping my mouth shut! And, sadly my vision didn't come to pass. However, if you absolutely *must* share your vision, please make sure this individual is of precious like faith. In the book of Ecclesiastes, scripture explains that a threefold cord isn't easily broken. In other words, girlfriend, an agreement establishes a word. (Deut. 19:15) You can either agree with someone you know will not care about your vision—"Maybe you're right. I shouldn't do it." Or, you can share the details concerning your vision with someone who genuinely cares enough to encourage you to follow your heart, "I believe God! I'm going to do this!" Discern! Discern! No matter what anyone else may think, feel, or believe. You keep right on trusting God's Word! Do not be moved! Stand on His Word!

Numbers 23:19 reads:

> **God is not a man, that He should tell or act a lie, neither the son of man, that He should feel repentance or compunction [for what He has promised], Has He said and shall He not do it? Or has He spoken and shall He not make it good? (AMP)**

Whatever the need, our Heavenly Father has it! He's a God of abundance! You've been set apart. (Acts 20:32) Girlfriend, you're special in the eyes of God. His grace is able to strengthen you spiritually, mentally and physically. It is *He* who gives you the ability to get wealth. (Deut. 8:18) Include spiritual aerobic exercises in your daily routine so the Word can live on the inside of you. While you're doing what is necessary in the natural to bring your dreams to pass, God is putting His super on your natural. (Deut. 30:14) (Rom. 10:8)

Faith without action isn't faith at all. Faith operating in your head doesn't give God anything to work with. So dig in your heels! One! Two! Three! Four! Elevate your faith! If no one else believes in your dreams, who cares? I encourage you to stay focused. Keep hope alive in the promises of God. Stabilize your faith by securing it with an unwavering heart. Shut those envious, non-believing people up! And, you know exactly who *they* are. They're the family members who think the house you currently live in is good enough. They're the ones who try to convince you not to apply for a new position opening on your job. Now, I'm probably going to be in big trouble! They're the folks at church who refuse to believe your marriage is really as happy as you claim it is. I could go on and on. Do you get my point? Every female reading this book has come in contact with people like the ones I've mentioned. And yes, *they* could very well be Christians. Did I say that?

Job 8:22 reads:

> **Those who hate you will be clothed with shame, and the tents of the wicked shall be no more. (AMP)**

Girlfriend, why not give those doubting Thomases and Thomasinas something to really talk about! Stay on course. Confess your faith. Speak your faith into fruition. When those same negative

Go Beyond Your Dreams
(Live Them!)

people see you living out your dreams, *they* will want to hear more about your God, and your faith! Success achieved God's way is another testimony to win a non-believer to Christ. I'm not telling you to shut people up in a boastful, arrogant way. First, foremost, and always, to God be the glory! What I'm simply trying to show is by acting on faith, *they* will see the God you serve is faithful to His Word. It'll give a clearer understanding why you weren't moved by anything they had to say. Negative feelings have a way of rubbing off. Spirits of gloom and doom long for companionship. Taking on the spirit (character) of another isn't as strange as it probably sounds. Let me give you an illustration so you won't think I bumped my head.

You run into an old acquaintance (hadn't seen her for months) at the supermarket. Instead of letting you finish grocery shopping (in peace), she starts telling you all about her financial problems. You politely listen, all the while silently scolding yourself for not ducking down the canned food aisle before she recognized you. As Gabby continues murmuring how much money she doesn't have, you stand behind your cart wishing you did the shopping yesterday instead of putting it off. Temporarily lost in your thoughts, you suddenly realize Gabby has gone from murmuring about a lack of money to complaining about people getting on her nerves at work. She proceeds to tell you about her three unruly kids, the lazy spouse, and the next door neighbor's barking dog. Somehow through all that you managed to keep smiling and nodding, but enough already! You slowly start to push your cart in the opposite direction. After listening to all of that negative mumbo-jumbo, your mind goes into overload. As you resume shopping your mind starts to wander.

A nice school age boy comes to the counter to bag your groceries. He looks to be about the same age as your 14 year old. Now you're wondering what's going to happen if there isn't enough money saved to send your teens to college. The check out cashier smiles. You return the smile, quickly diverting your eyes to the register. As you watch the grocery bill approach $200.00, lately, you find yourself feeling that there's hardly any money left over from your paycheck. Plus, you've been meaning to talk to your spouse about a family vacation. But he never wants to do anything fun. Then your mind kicks it up a notch. You're now questioning whether you'll be able to get your college degree so you can start your own business. Out of frustration, you shove the debit card back inside your purse and wheel your cart to the nearest exit.

Do you see what just happened? The enemy messed with your head! On the drive home he has you thinking the complete opposite of what you believed God was going to do for you and your family. Before the clerk could finish checking you out of the market, your old acquaintance's woe-is-me spirit rubbed off on you. As you leave the market

Go Beyond Your Dreams
(Live Them!)

parking lot, you utter, "I don't know why I bother. Things aren't going to change." Girlfriend! Hold it right there! Don't let your mind get your mouth in trouble! Those very words can hinder your move forward. (Job 15:5-6) Shake off that negative spirit! The same kind of urgency we put forth calling on the Lord during times of trouble is the same kind of tenacious spirit needed to maintain faith. If we truly believe God is able, we can't be moved by our senses. We can't see what we want to see. We can't hear what we want to hear. And, we definitely can't say whatever we feel like saying.

Reminding ourselves who we are according to God's Word is a learned behavior joined by a determined attitude. Spiritual exercising becomes a necessary discipline enforced by courage. Whenever you start to feel you've been waiting a long time, don't move! Hang in there! The ways of God are unlike the ways we (humans) do things. (Isa. 55:8) Our Heavenly Father is about doing things decently and in order. You mustn't become frustrated by what you're seeing in the meantime. Remain steadfast allowing God to work in the spirit realm on your behalf. (I Cor. 14:40) God will not half-heartedly (no interest), give His daughters any ole' thang. He will only give His absolute best. Which by the way, God's best in no way compares to what we perceive as the best of life. When we wait upon the Lord, faith teaches us patience. I'll admit when I'm waiting on God it's hard being patient. But wait I do because I know the answer to my prayer is already done. I can't be moved by my circumstances. Instead of complaining, I've learned to praise God anyhow! He promises to bring me through any crisis—big or small. God is worthy of my praises! Girlfriend, don't only praise God when He blesses you; praise Him when you're going through the wilderness! You have God's Word that you're equipped to overcome anything that would try to hold you back. Don't move! (Ps. 149:2-5) Try not to let a single day go by without giving God praise. He loves the praises of His people!

During the latter months of my marriage, I not only trusted God to come through for me, I expected Him to. As unhappy as I was at the time, do you think I felt like praising God? No! Girlfriend, I didn't feel like opening my mouth! My marriage was disintegrating right before my very eyes. I was angry! I couldn't understand why this was happening to me! Praising God was the last thing I wanted to do. But I forced myself! In spite of every wacky situation that was going on around me, deep down in my heart, I knew I was coming out victorious! I didn't know how God was going to do it, and I didn't worry about it either. I didn't want to risk taking matters into my own hands, so I asked God to give me peace (His peace) to endure. Then I got out of His way!

Go Beyond Your Dreams
(Live Them!)

Psalms 34:19 reads:

Many evils confront the [consistently] righteous, but the Lord delivers him out of them all. (AMP)

Whenever trouble parks itself on your doorstep, that's not the time to keep silent, shout HALLELUJAH! If you're expecting God's supernatural assistance, give Him praise anyhow! Here's a nugget for you. God won't force us to praise Him. But I guarantee once you dry your tears, lift your eyes toward Heaven and raise your hands in praise, you'll feel better. Hallelujah is the highest praise! This one word (Hallelujah) can transform your attitude. The next time a situation has you walking around in a fog, shout Hallelujah anyhow! Something about that word makes you feel spiritually stronger. (Ps. 105:2; 135:1) Praise increases faith. Praising God lifts our spirits. It keeps our heart on the defense protecting us against negative energies.

Let me tell you something else about myself. I like to think I'm a pretty good singer in the privacy of my home. Stop laughing! I'm always singing along with the latest Christian CD's, so I keep my voice fined tuned. Okay! Stop laughing! I think I sound pretty good harmonizing with *Yolanda Adams* and a few other female recording artists. Girlfriend, God doesn't care whether my singing voice is good, not-so-good, or downright terrible! It's all music to His ears. The point is, He wants me to give Him praise!

Psalms 63:3-7 reads:

> **Because Your loving-kindness is better than life, my lips shall praise You. So will I bless You while I live; I will lift up my hands in Your name. My whole being shall be satisfied as with marrow and fatness; and my mouth shall praise You with joyful lips. When I remember You upon my bed and meditate on You in the night watches. For You have been my help, and in the shadow of Your wings will I rejoice. (AMP)**

Do not be moved! If there's one thing I've learned in my faith-walk, is that you must have tough skin. The very idea that another human being can approach you and knock you for a loop with their words is reason enough to develop tough skin. Until we fully understand how important it is that we learn to separate the good words from the not-so-good words we hear on any given day, we're bound to digest what we hear. And, everybody knows you can't buy into everything that you hear. Take me for instance. Now that I know, that I know how powerful it is to have a heart built up in faith, and not walking around with faith in my head, I no longer allow people to say whatever he or she may be feeling at a particular moment. I'm quick to defend my space. Why? Because I had to learn the hard way that people flatter with their mouths while their hearts are

Go Beyond Your Dreams
(Live Them!)

speaking something entirely different. I was the morning joke in the coffee room at work for wanting to become a published author. The very same co-worker I thought I could trust was laughing behind my back! She didn't know I knew it, but I did. It didn't feel good to be the joke of the month. But what happened wasn't all bad. It taught me to stop being a blabber mouth (boasting was more like it) on my job with people who could've cared less about my dreams.

While growing in my Christian faith, I began praying, asking God to give me discernment, as well as His wisdom to know when someone is talking junk, or speaking from an honest heart. Girlfriend, smiling faces *really* do tell lies. That's not just a popular song recorded back in the day. It's for real. How many times have you experienced someone smiling and grinning in your face, going along with everything you were saying, only to have what you thought was spoken in secret shared with people you didn't want knowing your business?

The bottom line is this. Watch what you say. Watch what you're saying in front of people. Know when to speak. And, learn how to weed out the positive from the negative. If success and prosperity are to become a part of our lives, we must develop better skills in listening and speaking. They play an intricate part in keeping our hearts grounded in faith.

*Go Beyond Your Dreams
(Live Them!)*

Chapter 5
The Promises of God Are Meant For You

May the Lord, the God of your fathers, make you a thousand times as many as you are and bless you as He has promised you! (AMP)

Deuteronomy 1:11

Unlike promises made by man, the promises of God can never be broken. If God said it, He's going to do it! God cannot lie. An act of faith demonstrates we are committed to trusting Him with an expectation of receiving an answer to our prayer request(s). By making time to fellowship more with God, you can help alleviate your situation. You may have to make the sacrifice of turning off the television a few days out of the week. Or, quite possibly you may even need to ignore the ringing of the telephone. The reading of God's Word serves as instructions for our lives. Take advantage of its teachings because the Word of God can never be exhausted. Success happens when we're obedient, doing what the Word says. It's not just about listening to the pastor every Sunday. Your pastor ministers the Word, but it's up to you to apply it to your life. God has given us His promise to never leave us, nor forsake us. (Heb. 13:5) It's comforting to know that no matter what, we are never alone. God promises to be right by our sides while we're going through the good, as well as the not so good.

I previously mentioned the covenant promises exchanged between God and Abraham were not meant for Abraham alone. Those very same promises belong to you! God has a strong desire for prosperity and success to be upon His chosen people.

Galatians 3:29 reads:

> **Also, since you are Christ's family, then you are Abraham's famous "descendant," heirs according to the covenant promises.** (THE MESSAGE)

God promised we'd be blessed in the city, and blessed in the field. When we are adopted into God's Kingdom, everything He has becomes accessible to us. God loves us so much that He sent His only begotten son from heaven down to earth for the redemption of man. Jesus paid the ultimate price for our sins by laying down His life. If God loves His only Son, (Jesus) enough to sacrifice Him unto death, yet raised Him again, how much are you willing to believe He will make provisions for you too? Our God is no respecter of people. He loves you as much as He loves Jesus.

Go Beyond Your Dreams
(Live Them!)

Romans 8:32 reads:

> **He who did not withhold *or* spare [even] His own Son but gave Him up for us all, will He not also with Him freely *and* graciously give us all [other] things? (AMP)**

Girlfriend, God promised to supply your *every need*. Every problem, every challenge, or any nuisance situation that comes along, your faith is capable of bringing victory! The enemy was defeated by the most powerful man to ever walk the earth—Jesus Christ! The enemy has no power over you, or your loved ones! Don't believe the hype! The devil ain't all that! You are more than a conqueror! (Rom. 8:37) By faith, all of God's promises belong to His chosen children.

Here comes another 'but' clause. But you must develop an intimate relationship with God to hear His voice. Even though we may dream of leading an abundant lifestyle, if we're not hearing from God for clarity, we're bound to mess up. However, the good news is, God blesses our mess too. He takes everything and turns it around for our good. He's a God of many chances. Your success will be rewarded over and over again when you diligently make time to get alone with God. That's where the idea for sitting down to prioritize your time can serve as a blue print for keeping you on track. Be mindful of time, and how it's managed. Just think. The days of having to borrow money from creditors will long be a forgotten memory. Creditors won't be harassing us on our jobs with threats of turning us over to a collection agency. The bank will not send intimidating letters threatening to foreclose on our homes. We won't have to park our cars at a relative's house out of the fear of repossession. Our God is able to supernaturally release us from financial bondage when we trust Him out of hearts filled with faith! (Deut. 15:6) (Jer. 30:8)

Girlfriend, God even promised to give us real estate. That plug was for the single woman sitting around waiting on a man to buy her a house. You can buy your own! Write down the vision for what you want! Then find yourself some pictures! Show the enemy what God will do on your behalf. (Deut. 6:10-11; 19:8) Trust God to keep every promise He's ever made because God takes delight in your prosperity. Daily reading of His Word helps us familiarize ourselves with the promises God speaks of all throughout the Bible. When we go through storms, God promised to give us rest. There's no need to stress ourselves when trouble comes along.

I Kings 8:56 reads:

> **Blessed be God, who has given peace to his people Israel just as he said he'd do. Not one of all those good and wonderful words that he spoke through Moses has misfired. (THE MESSAGE)**

Go Beyond Your Dreams
(Live Them!)

Jesus Christ is another promise from God sent into the earth to redeem man from his iniquities and sins. God raised Jesus from the grave for our benefit to save us from spending eternity in hell. (Acts 13:23; 13:30) Jesus Christ is God's greatest promise of redemption available to all of mankind! Acceptance of Jesus into our hearts opens our eyes to see He is a light shining through all the dark places in our lives. Jesus became our ever living, everlasting hope for truth and salvation. *God gave the world His son.*

Girlfriend, hear me when I say, God has the almighty power to turn around what appears to be defeat, blessing you with the victory! (Jer. 33:6-9) As the seed of Abraham, the promises of God were made available to you through righteousness that comes by faith.

Romans 4:13 reads:

> **That famous promise God gave Abraham—that he and his children would possess the earth—was not given because of something Abraham did or would do. It was based on God's decision to put everything together for him, which Abraham then entered when he believed.** (THE MESSAGE)

Remain steadfast in strengthening your faith. Don't waver. You have God's Word in those moments of distress. God will give you rest (assurance) within your spirit, and in your physical body (worry and stress free). (Ps. 16:9) (Isa. 14:3)

Psalms 94:12-13 reads:

> **How blessed the man you train, God, the woman you instruct in your Word, providing a circle quiet within the clamor of evil, while a jail is being built for the wicked. (THE MESSAGE)**

CHAPTER 6
TRUST IN GOD'S UNFAILING LOVE

The fear of man brings a snare, but whoever leans on, trusts in, and puts his confidence in the Lord is safe and set on high.
(AMP)

Proverbs 29:25

Who hasn't trusted in someone, or some thing at one time or another? We trust our families not to hurt, or disappoint us. We trust our best friend to keep our confidence. We trust our employer to pay us. I cannot begin to name all of the things we place our trust in. Be honest. Ask yourself. Do I *really* trust God completely? The bottom line is this. Either we're going to trust God, or we're not. Three things occur when we apply faith: (1) belief, (2) trust, and (3) expectancy. That's what possessing heart filled faith means. You exercise your heart until you develop an attitude that no good thing will God withhold from you. (Ps. 84:11)

Possessing faith must become a major part of wanting to see positive results. God will definitely show up when He observes you trusting Him, trusting less in yourself, and others. People aren't always reliable. Truth be told, there's many a woman who've been disappointed by what someone else did, or didn't do. Girlfriend, people are not the source to make dreams come true. God is! We can go to Him anytime. Morning, noon, and night. He doesn't return broken promises. God doesn't make lousy excuses. In the book of Isaiah, Chapter 65, verse 24 it tells us when we call upon the name of God, He answers our prayers before we've finished praying. We have the guarantee (promise) His Word will never return void. (Isa. 55:11) If God said He's going to do it, consider it already done! Far too often we miss what God predestined for our futures. That's not to say we weren't walking in faith. However, if our level of trust wasn't where it should've been, and faith was actually in our minds, well....

A display of trust reflects expectation. Possession of heart filled faith is serious business. Trusting God won't be any easier than retaining faith. What we don't need at this crucial point in our lives are negative suggestions or opinions from others, especially when they could actually care less about our dreams.

I'm taking a chance here because I realize you may not like what I'm about to say. You could possibly put the book down right here. But I say this in love. Girlfriend, when you receive responses opposite of what you believe in relation to your vision and/or dreams, stop talking! Anything negative is not of God! Who told you that you have to disclose every vivid detail of your vision? Use wisdom!

Go Beyond Your Dreams
(Live Them!)

Please recognize (discern) that a negative reaction is usually an indication those people would rather see you fall flat on your face. You didn't stop reading, did you? I hope not!

Seriously. How can you think someone mouthing off against your dream is worthy of being a part of your vision? If they appear to be uninterested in what you're saying, they ain't the one! If they fall short on words of encouragement, they definitely ain't the one! It's perfectly alright to keep your vision between you and God. You'd do good to say nothing until it manifests itself. One more thing, if God hasn't led you to talk about the vision, then keep it to yourself until He tells you differently. Don't make my mistake.

I had an experience that took place years ago when I didn't know any better. I ran off with my mouth. Let me share my story. I'd met with a representative for a vanity press publisher. I opened my big mouth at work, bragging to my co-workers that I had written a book. I told them everything— blah, blah, blah. This office worker (me) was getting her first book published! Long story short. It never happened! Turns out I got my hopes (not faith) up for nothing. The publisher wanted me to fork over a lot of money to have them publish my book. I said, "*no thanks!*" I went back to square one. I began writing query letters and soliciting publishing houses. I couldn't admit it back then, but that book was awful!

There wasn't a publisher on the planet who wanted my book!

Shortly after opening my big mouth, I was greeted with the number one question on all of my co-workers minds. *"When's your book coming out?"* This went on for almost a year. But here's the clincher. One morning two of my co-workers didn't realize I was in the bathroom. I overheard them talking about me behind my back. One of the women commented laughing, *"I knew she didn't write a book. She always tries to outdo the rest of us!"* Then the other co-worker chimed in, *"She's gonna be here working with the rest of us!"* Their jeers hurt my feelings real bad! I quietly coward behind the closed stall door unnoticed. It didn't take a rocket scientist to figure out I'd made a huge mistake by shooting off my mouth. Needless to say, after that episode in the bathroom, I became a closet writer. With the exception of my immediate family and my dearest friend Jeannette, no one else would ever know how much I loved writing. I've since left that job. My dreams are no longer up for discussion outside of my small elite circle. It was a tough lesson to learn, but I GOT IT!

In the book of Genesis, Chapter 37, verses 5-28, is the story of Joseph. He's a perfect example of talking too much. Joseph shared his God-given dreams with his older brothers. And, why not? They were family. Surely if anybody would encourage Joseph, it would be his brothers ... right? Wrong! For

Go Beyond Your Dreams
(Live Them!)

starters, Joseph's brothers were jealous of his close relationship with their father. They hated Joseph because he was a dreamer, and in those dreams Joseph saw himself as an authority figure over them. His older brothers were not happy campers. Meanwhile, the enemy had seen their disgruntled attitudes, thereby seizing the moment. The enemy planted a devious idea in one of the brother's head. He simmered over it, entertaining the idea before telling the other brothers. After sharing his great idea (or so they thought), together the brothers plotted to make sure Joseph's dreams were laid to rest once and for all. They became conspirators working together to rid themselves of Joseph.

The plan was set. Unsuspecting Joseph found himself under attack at the hands of his older brothers. They threw him in a pit to leave him there to die, but guilt won over their callous hearts. The brothers pulled Joseph out of the pit, took his coat of many colors for evidence, and sold him into slavery. They returned home with Joseph's blood stain (animal blood) clothing, fabricating his death to their father. Finally the brothers were free! No more listening to Joseph and his big dreams! You'll have to read the story for yourself. But I wanted to make a point by telling you about Joseph. Despite the efforts of Joseph's brothers, years later when he matures into adulthood, Joseph's God-given dreams do come to pass! However, he doesn't achieve prosperous living without facing a lot of adversity along the way.

I've often wondered had Joseph kept his dreams to himself, would he have experienced so many obstacles before reaching his destiny. Perhaps not. But I believe what God shows us is exclusively for our eyes only, until He tells us when to share visions and/or dreams. Girlfriend, just because you desire prosperity doesn't mean everyone else does. There are a lot of people quite content to muddle through life. I know personally no one can deflate dreams quicker than a non-dreamer. I thought my co-workers had a good laugh at my expense that day in the bathroom. Pleeze! That was nothing compared to having a couple of family members look back at me cross-eyed from the slightest hint of wanting more out of my life.

A few years ago my pastor began ministering on faith and the things to watch out for. He explained faith-busters. Following his teachings I learned how to recognize the body language and zeroed in on a faith-buster's vocabulary. If they couldn't offer anything spiritually beneficial to me, I kept my distance. I still practice this today.

At 50-something, I don't need melodrama. And, I definitely don't want to surround myself with people who have a master's degree in stomping all over my faith for prosperity. Negative voices try to corrupt your mind, or influence your heart. Believe it, or not. What *they* don't know won't hurt them, but it could hurt you. It's most unfortunate that the very idea of someone having visions and dreams can be

Go Beyond Your Dreams
(Live Them!)

intimidating. And, more times than not, people respond negatively out of fear. Do like I do. Ignore them! Be encouraged to stay right where you are. Don't budge an inch! The last thing you need is to be out of position when God paves the way to golden opportunities. No matter how anyone else feels, keep trusting God!

So what if you haven't moved into a three and a half bath, six bedroom house with a three car garage nestled in a prestigious neighborhood. Trust God anyhow! With God, you can own the house of your dreams! You might be driving a car manufactured fifteen years ago, literally about to fall apart, making all sorts of strange noises. Trust God anyhow! With God you could soon be driving the car of your dreams! You may be in the same position, sitting behind the same desk when you started working for that company years ago. Trust God anyhow! Promotion and financial increase belong to you!

Mothers, you may not have the most well-behaved children. Trust God anyhow! If they have you for a mother, they can change! The love of your life may have put on a few pounds, and isn't as romantic since the children came along. Trust God anyhow! God can restore your husband back to the man you fell in love with!

Girlfriend, do you see where I'm going with this? Do you understand that all things are available when you have a heart of faith? (Ps. 73:28; 86:10) And, another thing. Don't be fooled by the physical appearance of another female.

Psalms 73:12 and 73:26 reads:

> **Behold, these are the ungodly, who always prosper *and* are at ease in the world; they increase in riches.**
>
> **My flesh and my heart may fail, but God is the Rock *and* firm Strength of my heart and my Portion forever.**
> **(AMP)**

I don't care if this woman wears a stylish new outfit to work everyday, keeps her hair and nails immaculate, and seems financially unaffected by the declining economy. Envy her not! She doesn't have *anything* that isn't attainable! Her seemingly worldly accomplishments aren't worth opening the door to a spirit of covetousness. And, don't tell me jealousy doesn't rise up on the inside of Christian women! We are human after all.

One Sunday I stepped inside the church sanctuary, only to see a woman wearing a dress I'd been waiting to go on sale. I was so jealous, I couldn't take my eyes off her! She was wearing my dress! A few days later I bought myself two pairs of the cutest wedge heel shoes to help ease the pain. Seriously though, women, we gotta learn to be content with what we have for the moment. I didn't

Go Beyond Your Dreams
(Live Them!)

say be satisfied. There's a big difference between the two. A satisfied woman will not step out of her comfort zone. A content woman looks beyond what's in front of her. So regardless how your life looks today, praise God anyhow! Your life as you know it is subject to change any minute.

While we're on the subject of envy, isn't it just like the devil to send a co-worker over to your desk gloating because her husband surprised her with a new faux fur coat. You sit there trying to remember when is the last time you even bought a coat that wasn't for one of the kids. Then to add insult to injury, your co-worker starts bragging she and hubby are going to St. Lucia for ten days on a second honeymoon. The enemy immediately plants images in your mind. *"She's married to such a considerate man. Don't you wish your husband did things like that for you?"* Suddenly those thoughts shoot feelings of envy straight to your heart. While you listen to Miss Thang, you're smiling, but you really want to claw her eyes out! See how the enemy makes you think about another female?

Girlfriend, so what if your honeymoon was the equivalent of a weekend get away? So what if you and hubby only look at pictures of the Caribbean Islands? Sure, he's been promising a romantic vacation ever since your first wedding anniversary, which was several years ago. So what? Then again, perhaps you're not married. Why is it lately seems like everywhere you turn another female is deliriously happy sharing the grand news of becoming engaged? The enemy puts a negative thought in your mind. *"At the rate you're going, if you don't soon get married, who's going to want you? You'll be too old."*

Can I tell you something? The truth is. It doesn't matter how glamorous someone else's life may appear on the surface, as a woman trusting in God, you have a much greater reward. Have you ever stopped to consider perhaps Miss Thang places her trust in all of her worldly possessions and nothing else? Don't be jealous! You have something money could never buy. You possess an unfailing love of God. Putting more trust in earthy treasures or within people, while electing to leave God out of the equation, doesn't require any faith. Be not deceived by appearances. Not one female trusting in God shall be abandoned. I suggest you smile, pretend you have to make a phone call, and send Miss Thang back to her own workspace!

Now, for my single girlfriends waiting for Mister Right, he's not coming! There is no such thing as Mister Right. However, there is a Mister Handpicked by God out there for you. That's the man you want to wait for. Girlfriend, don't settle for a counterfeit model when you can marry the cream de la crème. In other words. The grass ain't always greener over in the other neighbor's yard.

Go Beyond Your Dreams
(Live Them!)

Psalms 34:18-19 reads.

If your heart is broken, you'll find God right there; if you're kicked in the gut, he'll help you catch your breath. Disciples so often get into trouble; still, God is there every time.
(THE MESSAGE)

Remain fully committed (in your mind, heart and spirit), to doing things God's way. It can't be the way you think prosperity ought to be pursued. The way to prosperity has to be under the spiritual guidance and direction of God. Trust Him! Patience will have its way with you whether you like it, or not. Before a dream becomes a reality, you will have adapted to being patient when it comes to the things of God. He operates on an entirely different timetable.

We can kick, scream, and ball our eyes out, jump up and down throwing a big girl tantrum. "I want it! I want it now!" But God isn't giving up anything until He's ready. And you know what? When it's all said and done, God knows exactly when we're spiritually mature to handle everything He predestined for us. Your closet lined with pretty fur coats is closer than you realize. A wonderful loving man of God is being positioned and primed, especially for you. Wait on God.

Psalms 40:4 reads:

> **Blessed (happy, fortunate, to be envied) is the man who makes the Lord his refuge *and* trust, and turns not to the proud or to followers of false gods.** (AMP)

Girlfriend, start believing that the best is yet to come! The God we serve is able to perform all things! (Ps. 57:2) Trust Him at all times while He's working in the midst of your life. (Ps. 118:8) During tough moments when it seems like your faith is running low, hold on! God's coming to your rescue! He will not disappoint you! (Ps. 119:81; 125:1) We live on planet earth. There are going to be times (I can testify to this), when our spirit grows heavy. I've shed tears, battled with "why me?" and even thought I couldn't go another day waiting for my dream to manifest. But she who sows in tears will reap in joy! That's a promise from God! Never mind what *they* say! Who are *they* anyhow? Wait on the Lord! He doesn't mind when we get a little weary. God understands. What He does mind, is when we stay there too long with thoughts of giving up. Hang in there! God is faithful to His Word! (Ps. 30:5; 126:5)

Regardless whether you've entered a place where it feels like you can't take another disappointment, another heartache, another bad medical report, or another devastating experience, you're never without help. God is your defense. He'll

Go Beyond Your Dreams
(Live Them!)

rescue you every time your foot starts to slip. He promised to comfort us when our spirits grow heavy, weighed down emotionally by the pressures of this world. We must keep our eyes on Him no matter what challenges we encounter. It's all a part of life, but God is always right by our side. (Ps. 145:14) He promised to never leave us, nor forsake us. God wants to be a part of our daily lives. He sees everything that we go through down here on planet earth. Nothing escapes the tender, loving eyes of God. So never think He doesn't know, understand, or see what you're going through. Our pain is His pain. Our loss is His loss. When we're unhappy, God goes through those emotions with us.

Psalms 145:16-20 reads:

> **Generous to a fault, you lavish your favor on all creatures. Everything God does is right—the trademarks on all his works is love. God's there, listening for all who pray, for all who pray and mean it. He does what's best for those who fear him—hears them call out, and saves them. God sticks by all who love him, but it's all over for those who don't. (THE MESSAGE)**

I don't know how you picture success, but I see successful living as a woman who is steadfast, trusting the promises of God. Girlfriend, if you consistently do your spiritual aerobic exercises, they help combat fear. Continue strengthening your heart with God's Word. God has not given His daughters a spirit of fear. Remember, the enemy doesn't have any power over us!

II Timothy 1:7 reads:

> **For God did not give us a spirit of timidity (of cowardice, of craven and cringing and fawning fear), but [He has given us a spirit] of power and of love and of calm *and* well-balanced mind *and* discipline *and* self-control. (AMP)**

If you speak out God's Word declaring yourself to be more than a conqueror, nothing shall be impossible for you! Trust in God's Word without any fear of what a man, or another woman can do to you. (Ps. 56:4; 56:10-11) While you continue walking uprightly before God, He has promised to deliver you from difficult situations.

Ephesians 3:16 reads:

> **May He grant you out of the rich treasury of His glory to be strengthened *and* reinforced with mighty power in the inner man by the [Holy] Spirit [Himself indwelling your innermost being and personality]. (AMP)**

Girlfriend, a daily regimen of the truth (the Word) renews your mind, especially during those moments when you may need an extra boost to get

***Go Beyond Your Dreams
(Live Them!)***

started! There's no getting around feeding our hearts, and minds with the enriching nourishment of God's Word. We can trust the Gospel because His Word has already been settled in Heaven. (Ps. 119:89) I'd like for you to do something for me. Will you pause for a moment? Now, say these words aloud. *"Where do I want to see my life in five years?"* Please close your eyes for about fifteen seconds.

If your future doesn't look much different than what you see today, consider changing it. Do you want to know how to lead a whole, self-rewarding, and abundant life? Seek the Word of God. Do you want your circumstances to change? Read the Word of God. Do you want to have the character of a virtuous woman? Learn from the Word of God. If you don't have a Bible, invest in one. Girlfriend, it's my desire that not one female who's reading this book would perish (lose her soul), or forfeit her kingdom inheritance out of ignorance. The Word of God is literally a life-saver! Trust God because His love will never fail you!

Whenever you're feeling overwhelmed, remind yourself victory is yours through Jesus Christ. The enemy doesn't want me sharing this, but I'm going to tell you anyway. You have the upper hand! You are spiritually equipped to do *all* things through Christ who strengthens you! Glory to God! (Phil. 4:13) He's on your side. You have what it takes to defeat anything that gets in your way. Always remember, greater is He who lives on the inside of you, than he who is in the world! (I Jn. 4:4) How can you lose? Girlfriend, there are no failures in God! (Ps. 18:32; 27:1) (Heb. 13:6) There isn't a single situation or critical problem too hard for our Heavenly Father! (Gen. 18:4)

Matthew 19:26 reads:

> **But Jesus looked at them and said, With men this is impossible, but all things are possible with God.** (AMP)

In the book of Genesis there was a woman named Sarah. She was the wife of Abraham. God told Abraham that he and his wife Sarah would conceive a child. (Gen. 17:16) Abraham was 99 years old. Sarah was 90. Sarah overheard a conversation between Abraham and the Lord. She stood in the tent door listening as the Lord explained she would give birth to a son. (Gen. 18:10-12) She laughed. Sarah found it hard to believe she was going to get pregnant after years of desiring to have a baby. Sarah's mind wouldn't allow her heart (lacking faith) to remotely even consider the idea, an old girl like herself have a baby? Not! No way! Her biological clock had long since stopped ticking. In Sarah's disbelief, she couldn't understand all things were possible with God. She couldn't believe God was able to do exactly what He told Abraham He'd do.

Had Sarah been a woman stimulated by faith, she probably would've conceived Isaac soon after God visited Abraham. But in her heart, she couldn't believe for a baby although it had been Sarah's heart desire. For years she desperately wanted to be a mother. Unbeknownst to Sarah, her unbelief was a hindrance to the promise. Not only that, Sarah wanted a child so badly, she stepped out of God's Will. She manipulated Abraham into the arms of her handmaiden, Hagar. Sarah got this idea planted inside her head (by the enemy) to *make* things happen. Meanwhile, the larger Hagar's stomach stretched in her pregnancy, the more it became sheer torment for Sarah. She hated Hagar for doing exactly what she wanted. Following the birth of Ishmael, Sarah hated him too. Between Abraham's love for his son, and Hagar's presence, Sarah's spirit grew troubled. She wasn't the first, nor will she be the last woman to take matters into her own hands. When we don't trust God (wait for Him), we usually work ourselves into an emotional uproar with the outcome. If we're really honest with ourselves, we've all hated the end results when we leave God out of our plans. On occasion, I certainly thought God was taking too long to respond to a situation. That's when I decided to do things my way. Talk about making matters worse!

Don't let impatience bring you a counterfeit result. There isn't anything too hard for our God. We are never without His help at all times, through all things! (Heb. 13:5) God is our defense against whatever occurs in our lives. We don't need to help God. He's quite capable of handling things Himself. One thing's for certain. We can't believe in dreams one day and a day or two later start doubting them. We can't get excited listening to our pastor preach an uplifting message, only to wake up Monday morning, doubting faith really works. When you allow doubt to come into play, you know what? Girlfriend, you invite deception to have it's way with your thoughts, which ultimately effect your speech. As soon as you begin declaring the faith you have in God's Word, that's when the enemy shows up. He wants to do everything he can to punch holes in your faith. Many times problems and situations suddenly crop up because the enemy is afraid your determination will draw you closer to your destiny. He doesn't want to take any chance in you believing God's Word.

The enemy tries to plant doubt and confusion in your head the second you make a quality decision concerning faith. He hates our confidence in God's Word. God emphatically promised Sarah the desire of her heart—a baby. And what did she do? She let doubt flood her head with unbelief. Sarah was fully persuaded that she was far too old to be thinking about a baby, even if God did say it. She was convinced people were going to call her crazy for believing in the impossible. Well, Sarah started entertaining those thoughts. Instead of waiting (trusting) in what the Lord said, she got herself a surrogate mother. Sarah perceived her barrenness (difficult situation) as the end of her means. Sadly she couldn't conceive Isaac in the natural because Sarah was unable to conceive him in her heart (faith)

Go Beyond Your Dreams
(Live Them!)

first. When Sarah laughed at God's promise, in my opinion, she shot herself in the foot. Needless to say, years later Sarah was even older before God's promise came to pass. Sarah needed to mature spiritually in the things of God. He watched Sarah's heart (faith) change. It was then that God was able to do what He had promised Abraham. (Gen. 21:1-2)

Women (including me), have done what Sarah did. We say we trust God's Word, yet we allow the enemy to talk us out of receiving what God has for us. Sunday after Sunday we sit in church listening to our Pastors minister the Word. We faithfully read and confess God's Word. Then all it takes is for the enemy to use someone to cause us to second guess the measure of our faith. When God asks why we didn't wait a while longer, we give Him excuses. *"Well God, it's not that I didn't believe you. I thought you forgot. I didn't think my dream was ever going to come true, so I gave up."* You know what? God answers. *"All right."* As He steps away. It's not for you, or me to always try to figure out how God's going to do something. That's God's business to do as He pleases.

Philippians 4:19 reads:

> **You can be sure that God will take care of everything you need, his generosity exceeding even yours in the glory that pours from Jesus.** (THE MESSAGE)

Girlfriend, so long as you know who you are, and to whom you belong, the enemy does not have any power over you! God has set you apart for Himself. This means you're a special kind of woman. Whenever you call on Him in times of trouble, God hears you. Why be bombarded with problems weighing you down? Lay your prayer (petition) before Jesus. Then patiently wait, expecting faith to bring the result! (Deut. 14:2) (Ps. 27:14) Sarah's unbelief is a lesson to learn for all of us. We must try not to take matters into our own hands. (Ps. 9:9-10; 12:5-6)

There's a scene in the movie, *Gone With The Wind* that struck me for the first time only after having watched this movie about a gazillion times. The lead character, Scarlet O'Hara has returned to the land where she was born and raised. Following days of little or nothing to eat, she wanders outside to an abandoned potato field. Scarlet bends down in a tattered and worn dress to eat a potato, but it's spoiled. Unable to digest the rotten potato, Scarlet defiantly stands to her feet. It's in that moment of brokenness she angrily raises her fist toward Heaven. "As God is my witness! I'll never be hungry again!" she declares.

I realized for the first time, the instant Scarlet confessed those words, they became the driving force to overcome her adversity. Her words became life. Scarlet had enough sense to speak change into her life. And sure enough, a short time later she began to see light at the end of what had been a dark tunnel. Scarlet O'Hara proceeded to live out her fondest dreams. However, I'd also like to point out that while she may have overcome adversity, it didn't eliminate Scarlet from facing future struggles. I noted this heroine because Scarlet O'Hara demonstrates that if we are to overcome anything we must first determine within ourselves to fight! After all, we are world over comers! Quit focusing on the problem, especially when there's nothing you can do about it. Scarlet O'Hara had a tenacious spirit, and a well made up mind never to go hungry again.

Lack is an enemy. Whether it be lack of health or lack of finances. Lack is in direct opposition to freedom. Financial lack constantly keeps you from not having enough money to be a giver—a blessing. Overdue bills, maxed out credit cards, a mortgage or rent, a car note and other miscellaneous bills are traps of the enemy. When our paycheck no longer keeps up with the high cost of living, that's an enemy induced lack-attack! He's trying to deliberately wear us down spiritually. A broken spirit leads to hurt and anguish. Emotions run wild! It's not God's Will to watch His daughters struggling or jumping through hoops as a result of being distressed.

Psalms 18:47-48 reads:

> **The God Who avenges me and subdues peoples under me, Who delivers me from my enemies; yes,**

You lift me up above those who rise up against me; You deliver me from the man of violence. (AMP)

Keep your eyes, heart, and mind on the Lord. You know as well as I do sometimes certain situations have a way of causing us girls to take leave of our senses. Depending how severe the problem is, we can't think straight. That's why we have to put all of our trust in God. It's imperative that we develop the habit of learning to patiently wait on the Lord. Our Heavenly Father is well aware of what's going on in our lives. He gives us grace to withstand pressure from the enemy. Girlfriend, you've been equipped spiritually to whip the devil in Jesus' name! Open your mouth! It will only be a matter of time before all that distress is replaced by joy.

Psalms 34:19 reads:

Many evils confront the [consistently] righteous, but the Lord delivers him out of them all. (AMP)

It's vital that we read His Word everyday as part of our spiritual aerobic exercises. God's Word helps prepare us for the tough times. The Word teaches us how to say (aloud) the opposite of what our situation looks like for the moment. Unfortunately, if you have very little Word stored inside your heart, the enemy has an opportunity to take advantage of you. Remember he plants negative thoughts and images of failure in your mind. Once

Go Beyond Your Dreams
(Live Them!)

the enemy sees doubt has infiltrated your thought pattern, which ultimately affects your speech, he goes after your heart. The enemy wants to destroy every possible chance of faith manifesting your vision for prosperity.

Woman, God created you long before conception ever took place inside your mother's womb. So, I ask you. Who then knows you better than God, Himself? He knows your strengths. He knows all of your weaknesses. God knows what you're going to say even before you know what you're going to say. That's how awesome He is! Girlfriend, you are God's chosen treasure! He loves you! God is faithful to His Word! He wants to see you fulfill *His purpose* for your life! (Isa. 41:10) (Rom. 8:28-30) Bust the devil upside his head! Hit him with the sword of God's Word! Do you really want to know how you can keep the enemy under your feet where he belongs? Begin saying what God says about you....

I am more than a conqueror!	(Romans 8:37)
I have the victory through my Lord Jesus Christ!	(I Corinthians 15:57)
I am blessed and highly favored!	(Luke 1:28)

I am blessed coming in and blessed going out!	(Deuteronomy 28:6)
I am above and not beneath!	(Deuteronomy 28:13)
No weapon formed against me will prosper! And every false tongue that rises up against me shall be proven wrong!	(Isaiah 54:17)
Greater is He that lives on the inside of me, than he who lives in the world!	(I John 4:4)

Girlfriend, take authority over the enemy! Whenever he starts whispering lies of failure, open your mouth! If he sends someone in your face to do his dirty work for him, kindly excuse yourself. Walk away! I speak from experience. When despairing situations occur, you mustn't let them consume you. I woke up with a troubled marriage. I went to sleep with a troubled marriage. I was in despair every waking hour! Don't allow a problem to become a stumbling block around your pretty neck. Hang in there! God's love will sustain you. Trust Him! God promised He wouldn't allow you to suffer beyond what you can bear. (I Cor. 10:13)

Therefore, be steadfast in your heart (faith) believing God will turn your situation around. (Ps. 46:1; 54:4; 55:22) God has promised to bestow favor and honor upon you. It doesn't matter what kinds of

Go Beyond Your Dreams
(Live Them!)

problems you're dealing with today. Keep your heart firmly planted in God's Word. With a determined heart of faith, prosperous living is within reach for every area of your life. (Deut. 8:18) A heart fueled by faith can accomplish whatsoever you believe. You've been blessed with spiritual power to live out your dreams! Believe it's possible because God says with Him ***all things*** are possible!

Far too often we girls allow other women to express how, and what they see when looking back at us. That too interferes with God's plans for our lives. Instead of having total knowledge of what God has to say about us, we accept their opinions and advice. That's why it's very important to read God's Word to sustain our inner strength spiritually, mentally and emotionally. I don't know why females like putting down another female or making comparisons, especially when there's a vision or dream involved. It's almost as if she can discourage you from having what you say, then she's all the better for having set you straight. No, what she's done, and intentionally I might add, is try to crush your dream. But that's when you have to take on a pit bull mentality, and tell yourself you can do anything when your heart is in the right place.

It's true the heart is the life source that keeps us alive. However, it's also the part of our anatomy that God looks upon which determines our fate. Faith of the heart grows and matures until the time arrives to unveil the hidden desire of a woman. That's why

I'm a firm believer that what God has given you is specifically for you. It doesn't matter that another woman may share the same kind of idea. Her idea will not be your idea. Sure, you can collaborate on shared ideas, but if the two of you join forces, that idea will still reflect both of your personalities.

Life is made up of differences. That's what make all of us unique. Take for instance the movie industry. There are lots of movie stars in Hollywood, but none of those actors are the same. Each one brings something different to the screen. Regardless whether you have two female actresses playing the same type of character, one actress will play her character noticeably different from her co-star. The music industry is no different. You have your gospel singers, as well as secular singers. Not one is identical to the other, while they could sound very close in pitch and style.

As ordinary women striving for betterment in our lives, we've got to become more focused on trusting in God to guide and lead us to where He intended to take us. The problem is, we usually fail miserably at it. I can speak truthfully about myself. Time after time, I tried doing things the way I thought they should be done, only to mess up even more. So, why go through all that if it's as simple as consulting God through His Word. Why not pray for an answer and stand in faith until you get an answer? Why? Because we're human. Girlfriend, I'd be lying if I said I *always* get it right, because I don't! There

Go Beyond Your Dreams
(Live Them!)

have been instances when I knew for a fact God was telling me to do something one way, and I ignored Him completely.

So, again, I urge you to take doing spiritual aerobics seriously. Read! Pray! Seek God for direction. The only way to achieve His kind of success is to stay connected. Our hearts need to be replenished just as much as our minds are in constant need of renewal. If our thoughts are negative and doubtful, how can we expect our hearts to grow strong in faith? It cannot happen. The mind will override the heart every time.

Girlfriend, it doesn't matter how big you dream, just so long as you dream. God has given every female the ability to obtain her hearts desire whether it's fame and fortune, or to live out her years successful in other ways. The point is, God has provided us with the means and skills necessary to have what we say. It's time for all of us to not only desire change, but to physically see change taking place.

Go Beyond Your Dreams
(Live Them!)

CHAPTER 7
DEPENDING ON THE WISDOM OF GOD

The plans of the mind and orderly thinking belong to man, but from the Lord comes the [wise] answer of the tongue. (AMP)

Proverbs 16:1

Ever been in a situation where you didn't have a clue what to do? I have. There are too many times to count. If you are like me, you probably are uncertain whether to move forward, go left, go right, or stand still. Personally, I came very close to pulling my hair out a lot of times. But after thinking how ridiculous I'd look with patches of hair missing from my head, I broke up a few old mugs we no longer used instead. My kitchen floor was a mess, but throwing those mugs down to the floor sure made me feel better!

In a moment of indecisiveness, one or two things are apt to occur: (1) You make the wrong decision, or (2) You make the right decision. The wrong decision could be detrimental to your well being, and possibly those around you. A right decision could make all the difference in the world. But all is not lost. God sends the Holy Spirit to assist in our decision making. Your spirit confirms what you need to know by way of an inner prompting.

Romans 8:16 reads:

> **God's spirit touches our spirits and confirms who we really are. We know who he is, and we know who we are: Father and children.** (THE MESSAGE)

God speaks through the Holy Spirit to us from on the inside. The Holy Spirit tells us what God has told Him to say. I like to think of the Holy Spirit as my personal spiritual guide. He delivers God's direction to our thought pattern, or speaks to our heart (urging; prompting), to either go left, go right, or do nothing. God gives each one of us daily instructions byway of the Holy Spirit. When it comes to everyday off-sets, we certainly can use someone who is much wiser than we are to make rational decisions. The Holy Spirit is that person to keep us level headed in times when we have no idea what, or how to handle a situation.

Romans 15:13 reads:

> **May the God of your hope so fill you with all joy and peace in believing [through the experience of your faith] that by the power of the Holy Spirit you may abound and be overflowing (bubbling over) with hope.** (AMP)

Go Beyond Your Dreams
(Live Them!)

According to God's Word, we as Christians (born again believers) are obligated to *listen* and *do*.

James 1:22 reads:

> **Don't fool yourself into thinking that you are a listener when you are anything but, letting the Word go in one ear and out the other.** (THE MESSAGE)

Now might be a good time to look at the list of priorities you wrote down. If you're sitting in front of a big screen television night after night, don't count on hearing much of anything. If you're always on the go-go-go, busy-busy-busy, how do you really expect to hear God tell you what to do next? Our spirit has got to be receptive in order to clearly hear the prompting of the Holy Spirit. His voice is soft. I can best describe it resembling that of a hushed whisper. Girlfriend, He isn't going to raise His voice to be heard over your favorite TV show. The Holy Spirit also brings things (thoughts) back to your memory. (Jn. 14:26) I'll give you a perfect example. Have there been times when perhaps you were about to plunge head first into something without clearly thinking things through? Suddenly you sense something on the inside urging you to do the opposite of what you were thinking? Almost immediately your spirit receives what you heard in your thoughts. That's a God-connection confirming in your spirit that the Holy Spirit has spoken. He brought a word from God to prevent you from messing up. That's why it's so important to have the guidance of the Holy Spirit everyday. Now bear in mind, the enemy also talks to us. That sly snake competes with the Holy Spirit for our attention. The enemy tries to trick us into going the wrong way. The Holy Spirit prompts us to do the right thing. They both have access to our minds. Wrong decisions can open the door to emotional defeat. If the enemy can get you to think, or feel nothing is ever going to change, he's gaining on you! Girlfriend, would you please slap the enemy upside his lying head! We don't think twice about smacking our husbands, our children, or a boyfriend if we suspect they've lied. But we'll sit back allowing the devil to whisper one lie after another. We don't do one thing about it! That has to stop! Let him know that you know he's a liar!

The enemy comes to *steal, kill and destroy*! He'll make countless attempts to steal your inheritance. He's going to try to kill any vision God gives you. And, he will definitely try to destroy any opportunity of dreams ever coming to fruition. When it comes to making life altering decisions that not only effect you, but effect everyone around you, use wisdom. Don't be too proud to ask your Heavenly Father for help. Then prepare your heart to hear. The wrong voice can lead you to make hindering decisions. There is nothing more embarrassing than to boast in yourself and have that thing turn around and blow up in your face. Prideful boasting from a

*Go Beyond Your Dreams
(Live Them!)*

heart fueled by a big ego isn't smart. You're not trusting in God. You're trusting in yourself. Or even worse, you accept advice from an unreliable source, instead of waiting—listening for clear direction from the Holy Spirit.

Proverbs 3:21 reads:

> **Dear friend, guard Clear Thinking and Common Sense with your life; don't for a minute lose sight of them.**
> (THE MESSAGE)

God is working on His timetable. Not ours. Allow God all the time He wants to set everything in its proper order. Being spiritually positioned where God wants us to be has a lot to do with where we are right now. We just may not be prepared spiritually or mentally for where God wants to take us. Permit Him to re-adjust you, and your life. God has the inside scoop when it comes to removing unproductive things, and non-productive people out of our lives. I'll be the first to admit, it's never easy letting go of people. It's not any easier letting go of certain things. However, we must learn to recognize what God is doing when familiarity starts to take on a different look. We need to understand why He's pulling us away from what we've grown accustomed to. A discerning spirit has the capability to rationalize what's taking place in ones life.

Isaiah 55:8-9 reads:

> **I don't think the way you think. The way you work isn't the way I work. God's Decree, "For as the sky soars high above the earth, so the way I work surpasses the way you work, and the way I think is beyond the way you think."** (THE MESSAGE)

If you disclose the details of your vision to anyone who is nosey enough to listen (everybody isn't interested), then girlfriend prepare yourself. The enemy will set you up. He'll send people to harass you practically every time they see you. These folks have slippery tongues! *"So what's been going on since I saw you last? I was in the mall last week. I looked for your new store. When did you say you were opening your boutique? You're not having problems trying to get financing...are you?"*

Girlfriend, don't get mad. You should've kept your mouth zipped! Discretion isn't always a bad thing to follow. I'm thankful God doesn't think like me. I'm even more thankful He doesn't handle situations the same way I do. If I live to be 200, He's so much wiser than I could ever be. But this was something I gradually learned through the reading of His Word. I matured (spiritually) into keeping my mouth shut. Please, don't make the mistake of sharing your visions and dreams with just any ole' body. Ask God for His input before you say anything.

Go Beyond Your Dreams
(Live Them!)

Take it from me, people who lack vision seldom relate to what you want them to see. Save yourself the aggravation. If you didn't hear the Holy Spirit give His okay to share, then say nothing.

There aren't many things we can depend on these days, but we can always depend upon the wisdom of God. I depended on a company where I worked for X number of years. I planned to retire at age 65. I thought how great it would be to relocate to a warmer climate (Delaware gets cold), and live out the remainder of my years happy as a clam. Well things changed. After eighteen years, the job and the people got on my nerves. I resigned. I started working again in a couple of weeks. I was employed at this job a little over a year when I met my husband. We got married. I moved to Atlanta to live with him. A year later we relocated back to my home town. Nine years later we divorced. At fifty-something, I view early retirement entirely different than I did in my mid-30s. I question if there will be money in Social Security by the time I'm old enough to receive it. I also question will it make a difference where I live, just so long as I can afford to eat and keep a roof over my head. What can we really depend on, except the goodness of God.

I know, you're knowledgeable of the number of mergers, takeovers, the bankruptcy boom, and downsizing of large conglomerates that have resulted in job lay-offs across the country. The instability of this economy effects all of us. That's why we must learn early on how to depend and trust in God to be our major source for everything. God wants us to look upon Him for provision for prosperous living. Girlfriend, if God has given you a vision or a dream, let me encourage you to pursue it with a vengeance! That's where your prosperity is.

Naturally, I could go on and on about the way I used to think before I became a Christian, but why bore you? Looking back, I now know in the good ole' daze, I didn't understand many things. But then again, how could I? God wasn't included in any of my plans. For the most part, I figured things happened because I made them happen. Back then my mindset revolved around me, myself, and I. The only source I knew of was me. Not only was I living under the influence of ignorance, my soul was in danger of going to hell! I thank God for my life-long friend (more like a sister), Jeannette. She didn't let up on me until I finally accepted Jesus Christ as my Lord and Savior. There was a reason why she and I became best friends as young children. Our early friendship was a God setup. It's not God's Will that any of us should perish, but have eternal life. He will use others to see that His plans for salvation are carried out.

Psalms 65:3-4 reads:

> **Iniquities *and* much varied guilt prevail against me; [yet] as for our transgressions, You forgive *and* purge them away [make atonement for them**

Go Beyond Your Dreams
(Live Them!)

and cover them out of Your sight]! Blessed (happy, fortunate to be envied) is the man whom You chose and cause to come near, that he may dwell in Your courts! We shall be satisfied with the goodness Your house, of Your holy temple. (AMP)

While we're in the earth, God wants us to lead productive, rewarding lives. Every morning I thank Him for waking me up with a stable mind. Why? Because in the days of my youth it was *only* the grace of God who kept me from premature death. At fifteen I faced death. But for His grace, I'm still here! At sixteen I ignored a luring to death. But for His grace, I'm still here! At twenty-five I came close to death's door again. But for His grace, I'm still here! So I'm not ashamed to say, *"Father God, I love You!"* When I think how far He's brought me, I must say, *"thank You!"* Even when we act out of the flesh ignoring the call of God, He loves us so much, that He protects us even though we don't acknowledge Him. I'm grateful God still forgives us despite our human ways.

When I was twelve years old, I discovered my God-given desire for writing. The enemy tried to snuff me out early in my youth because he knew if I ever came into an understanding of my destiny, one day I'd possess what God preordained over my life. Sure, I sowed my wild oats when I was younger. I had a lot of fun while I was doing what I was doing too! Sometimes I stop to think about how much time has lapsed. I tell myself too much time has passed between then and now for me to waste another precious minute doing nothing. Girlfriend, are you beginning to get the picture? The enemy does everything he can to prevent us from having what God planned for us before we were born. But thank God it's never too late to follow the visions and dreams He purposed for us. Now don't get it twisted. The mercy and grace of God doesn't mean it's okay to do wrong (knowing to do right), with the mindset God will forgive whatever you might feel big enough to do. Yes, God does forgive us of our sins and transgressions. But let's not forget. He also knows you better than anyone else. What I'm trying to simply say is this; God is well informed ahead of time when we're going to act out of disobedience.

Can you recall when you were a little girl growing up how you couldn't hide anything from your mother because she already knew you were lying? It's pretty much the same way with God. There is nothing hidden from Him. We can all be thankful He provides grace over our lives during those fleshy moments. In other words, He gives us what we need (grace) to get our act together. (Eph. 2:8) However, grace doesn't automatically qualify us for a license to do whatever we please, to whomever we please, operating out of the flesh.

Go Beyond Your Dreams
(Live Them!)

I Peter 2:16 reads:

[Live] as free people, [yet] without employing your freedom as a pretext for wickedness; but [live at all times] as servants of God. (AMP)

Our God is all seeing. He's all knowing. God is Omniscient. There are times when we're not as strong as we might like to think. It comes as no surprise to God. He already knows it. That's why He instructs us to bring everything to Him in prayer. (Ps. 55:22) (I Pet. 5:7) Our Heavenly Father expects our dependency to be upon Him. Not solely upon ourselves. Not upon other people. Dependent upon Him. God is fully aware of the ways of His children. He knows what's best for us. Through knowledge of His Word, we learn how to depend on God. It's a learned behavior. Submitting to His Will doesn't happen overnight. Let's be honest. We barely want to submit to anyone. We learn how to do it.

The sooner we start depending less on other people we can begin leading purposeful lives. That's what I said! Stop putting pressure on the people in your inner circle, especially your loved ones to make *your* dreams come true! Leave your husband alone trying to make him see your vision. He'd rather watch a basketball game on TV! Give those kids a break looking up information for you on the internet! They've got homework to do on the computer. Why don't you sign up for a beginner's computer course at the nearest college? Then you'll be able to figure out the internet to research information for yourself! That's all I'm going to say about that. And, I said that in love.

Girlfriend, if your desire is to own and operate a florist shop, learn everything there is to learn about flowers, plants, business plans, proposals, and how to operate a successful business. Once you've educated yourself, open that florist shop. Depend on God to help you make your way. Your family and friends shouldn't be made to suffer because they're not at your every beck-n-call to assist in bringing your vision to fruition. Girlfriend, you are responsible for birthing forth your dreams.

We can never depend on God too much! There's no such thing as coming before Him too much, or too often. He's the Almighty God, the possessor of heaven and earth. He wants His daughters calling upon Him the same way we call and nag our earthly fathers. Don't let the enemy fill your head, trying to convince you, God gets tired of us. It's another one of the devil's lies. Feel free to call on God anytime. Day or night. He never slumbers nor sleeps. In the book of Hosea, it says the people of God are destroyed for a lack of knowledge. Learning to depend more on God is one of the smartest things we can do in our good fight of faith.

Everyone of us has been imparted with a unique talent and/or gift to do something constructive in our lives that glorifies God. Before we are born,

Go Beyond Your Dreams
(Live Them!)

dreams are tenderly tucked inside of us waiting to be discovered. Have you ever listened to famous people declare at a young age they knew exactly what they were going to do as adults?

Many successful individuals have testified they didn't know how or when, but they subconsciously knew one day they'd become the prosperous person they are today. Those are the people that made their discovery early on, and refused to let their passion elude them. Whether it was faith or hope that ushered in their prospering futures, they believed a successful life was attainable for them to achieve. The enemy tricks a lot of females telling them the world has enough gifted and talented people in the earth already. Shut up devil! There's plenty of room for you too! Girlfriend, the mere fact you have a desiring heart means there's a place of significance on the planet for your dream to be shared. That's the enemy's strategy of planting negative thoughts in your mind. He sets out to stop you before you can get started. There are new Christian authors getting their manuscripts published everyday. Nevertheless, it didn't discourage me from making *my way prosperous*!

A couple of years ago I was watching a well-known minister on Christian TV. My ears perked up when I heard these words. He said (I'm paraphrasing) *"all of us have varying degrees of ministry built on the inside of us."* He proceeded to explain. *"The thing that you love doing that makes you happy when you do it, is your ministry. That's what you were born to do."* Wow! Suddenly it made perfect sense why I never got far away from writing. Throughout my adult life I ran into a lot of detours, but I always found my way back to writing. Girlfriend, do you love singing? Who do you think gave you that beautiful voice? There will never be too many gospel singers expressing their love and devotion for the Lord. Do you realize your unique, individual singing voice could very well minister in such a powerful way, the words of your songs will lead people to Christ? In the meantime you'll prosper doing what you love to do, while winning souls to Christ.

Perhaps you're a woman with a distinctive eye for color coordination. Has your talent for decorating stirred the attention of others when they visit your home? Why not put that gift to the test? Volunteer to decorate a room for a friend. Enroll at a nearby college to further pursue a professional career in interior design. Your talent could possibly lead you into homes in dire need of salvation. Doing what you love has the potential to lead you to limitless possibilities for prosperity!

Whether it's a gift to sing, decorate, write, arrange flowers, paint, act, dance, own a boutique, own a fleet of limousines, fly jet planes, open a restaurant, or whatever vision God gave you, **LIVE IT!** Look to God as your source to help you achieve the dreams (passion) He placed on the inside of you.

Go Beyond Your Dreams
(Live Them!)

Your desire for success came from God. One of His promises in the Bible says God will give us the desires of our heart. (Ps. 37:4; 38:9)

Psalms 21:2 reads:

> **You have given him his heart's desire and have not withheld the request of his lips. Selah [pause and think of that]!** (AMP)

There comes a time when we must search deep within ourselves. That time is now. I don't care how old or young you are. Examine yourself. Uncap those unique qualities God gave you. Tap into your gifts and talents. Pursue them! Follow your heart! Girlfriend, you can do one or two things. You can either let your visions/dreams lay dormant, or you can make a quality decision to give birth to them! Shift your mind to a place where you become completely dependent upon God. Remain steadfast with an unwavering heart of faith! A very wise man once spoke these encouraging words. *"For where your treasure is, there will your heart be also."* That wise man was Jesus!

That which brings joy to your soul, and peace to your spirit is what you were born to do. Unlock those hidden treasures on the inside of you waiting to be discovered. Believing is seeing (through spiritual eyes), not the other way around. You don't wait till you see it (with natural eyes), to believe it. Through faith you believe for the impossible taking place (in the spirit realm) in your life right now. With God in the midst of your gifts, visions, talents, and dreams, no man can stop what He already has planned for you. God is just waiting for you to get up off the couch and accept the challenge to have what He says is available for you!

*Go Beyond Your Dreams
(Live Them!)*

CHAPTER 8
SHOW GOD YOU'RE TRUSTWORTHY

Let Your mercy and loving-kindness come also to me, O Lord, even Your salvation according to Your promise; then shall I have an answer for those who taunt and reproach me, for I lean on, rely on, and trust in Your word. (AMP)

Psalms 119:41-42

Girlfriend, I don't care how far away your dream looks in the future, don't give up on it! An attitude of self-defeat is exactly how the enemy wants you to react. You can't be fooled by what you see. The enemy is taking bets with his cohorts that you'll get frustrated. In fact the enemy is determined to make you discouraged. He plays dirty. However, giving up shouldn't be an option to the life of a Christian, especially if she believes faith released from her heart has the ability to bring her success. God has already given us the ability (faith) to get prosperity for every area of our lives! (Deut. 8:18) You can have what you say!

Matthew 19:26; 21:22 reads:

But Jesus looked at them and said, With men this is impossible, but all things are possible with God.

> **And whatever you ask for in prayer, having faith *and* [really] believing, you will receive.** (AMP)

Over and over, time after time, your faith will be tested. Success does not relinquish you from fiery darts. I kid you not. You will continue to be tested, even with your prospering lifestyle. In the meantime, should you start to feel sluggish, shake yourself. (Prov. 24:10) Confusion aroused by mistrust, and unbelief combined with a wishy-washy attitude will tie God's hands. Always remember. Without faith, it is impossible to please Him. (Heb. 11:6) As part of your spiritual aerobic exercises, renew your mind (the battleground) everyday, reading the Word of God. (Rom. 12:2) Girlfriend, only *you* can stop your dreams from coming to pass. As a child of God's Kingdom, what should it matter how long you might have to wait on the promises of God? Wait!

Lamentations 3:37-38 reads:

> **Who do you think "spoke and it happened"? It's the Master who gives such orders. Doesn't the High God speak everything, good things and hard things alike, into being?** (THE MESSAGE)

Throwing in the towel, or throwing up your hands because you're frustrated will get you nowhere with God. On the contrary, that displays a heart of distrust. Don't get mad with God when things don't quite work out as you planned. By seeking God's wisdom and direction, He will implement His plan for you. (I Thess. 4:12) I'm the first to admit, it's very easy to tell ourselves, "I can't do this!" Well, guess what? With a defeated mindset, seldom does anything get accomplished. So the next time you feel like you can't do something, say the opposite. Speaking positive isn't any easier for a Christian than it is for a non-Christian. We must program ourselves. But there's good news! God will deliver us from negative harmful speech! (Ps. 34:19)

Colossians 3:16 reads:

> **Let the word [spoke by] Christ (the Messiah) have it's home [in your hearts and minds] *and* dwell in you [all its] richness, as you teach and admonish *and* train one another in all insight *and* intelligence *and* wisdom [in spiritual things, and as you sing] psalms and hymns and spiritual songs, making melody to God with [His] grace in your hearts. (AMP)**

Read the Word to yourself aloud. Faith comes by hearing, and hearing, and hearing some more! (Rom. 10:17) God's Word supplies all the ability we need to get wealth. Girlfriend, how far you allow faith to take you focuses on a healthy spiritual attitude. Planting (reading) the Word in your heart on purpose builds confidence. (Jn. 15:7) Make your declaration (confession) aloud. Prophesy to yourself: "I WILL HAVE WHAT I SAY! IT'S ONLY A MATTER OF TIME BEFORE EVERYONE WILL SEE THE RESULTS OF MY FAITH!" Learn to speak into your life!

Here's a brief self-exam. I do this for myself from time to time. I figure we do self-breast exams in between mammogram check-ups, why not do a spiritual self-exam too? So, ask yourself. Can God *really* trust me to be a doer of His Word, and not just a hearer? (Jas. 1:22) Can He trust me to sow the Word into my heart? Do I genuinely live by faith, and not by sight?" (II Cor. 5:7)

In the previous chapter, I mentioned the similarity between the heart and the tongue. What is felt inside our heart is eventually expressed out of our mouths. That's why we mustn't become discouraged by what our lives look like today. Suddenly with God, everything is subject to change. His timing in no way resembles our sense of timing.

Luke 16:10 reads:

> **Jesus went on to make these comments: If you're honest in small things, you'll be honest in big things; If you're a crook in small things, you'll be a crook in big things.** (THE MESSAGE)

Girlfriend, how can I expect God to trust me with a big promotion, if I blatantly show disrespect

Go Beyond Your Dreams
(Live Them!)

for those in authority at my work place? How is He supposed to trust me with a new house, if I continue to neglect the home I have now by not keeping it cleaned? How can I be trusted with 'mo' money when I squander my paycheck at the mall instead of paying the bills? These are necessary questions we need to often ask ourselves.

I can recall as a child hearing my mother say, *"take care of what you have now so you'll always get better."* I was young, but she got my attention. I listened. And, you know what? Mom was right! I can honestly tell you for every large item I've obtained in my life it started out in a small way. Take my first car for instance. It was small, cute, and inexpensive. I treated that car like I paid a million dollars for it. Five years later when I got ready to trade in the car, the salesman couldn't believe how well I had taken care of it. I had no choice! My car had white leather seats! I took a lot of pride in that car. When it came time to negotiate a trade-in deal, I was rewarded. A few hours later I drove off the lot in a brand new larger car! I drove away without any financing. It wasn't until two weeks later when my car was financed through a bank. The dealership not only trusted me to remain in the state with their unsecured merchandise, I was now driving a more expensive, fully loaded car! My loan payments were $50.00 more than what I previously paid for the first car! It was a good life lesson what happened when I took care of what I had, regardless how inexpensive, or how small it was. Humble beginnings are a good thing.

Girlfriend, you might start out small, but that's okay. Don't let pressure from others have you confused that larger somehow means better. It's not true. If you listen to people, they'll have you purchasing things you have no business getting. Trying to keep up with the Joneses could lead you to serious debt! Are these people going to help you get outta debt? I think not! Small beginnings are opportunities to show God your gratitude. Let Him see how much you appreciate what He's given you already.

Job 8:7 reads:

And though your beginning was small, yet your latter end would greatly increase. (AMP)

Here's something you may not realize. Sometimes having more is overwhelming in a nonproductive sort of way. How so? Well, having more could catch you off guard (immaturely), if you've not been fully prepared spiritually. I'm sure you've heard the stories, or perhaps seen on TV where instant million dollar (some higher) winners have practically spent every dime of their millions within a short period of time. Why? Because they weren't prepared for sudden wealth.

Preparation could be something as simple as working every Saturday for one month. Overtime is

Go Beyond Your Dreams
(Live Them!)

an excellent way to demonstrate to God you'd diligently work long hours operating your business without murmuring and complaining. While everyone else is enjoying their weekend, you'll be working. Your actions also show an act of respect for those in authority. God then sees how unaffected you are working long hours, which self-employment usually demands of you. Girlfriend, please do not tell me you're concerned what your co-workers will say if they find out you're working on weekends. So what! Are you, or are you not trying to fulfill your destiny? Pleeze! Who cares if it looks like you're being taken advantage of, according to the opinion of a busy body co-worker? They're probably jealous cause your boss didn't ask them. If you're an employee with model work ethics, supervisors make note of you as a valuable employee. You're someone he/she can rely on to get to work on time, mind your own business, and get your work assignments finished while you're on the clock.

May I make a suggestion? Let that co-worker say whatever. Ignore them! You'll be raking in double-time pay for sacrificing your Saturdays. Didn't you petition God requesting financial increase? Well, He answered your prayers! Learn to recognize God-opportunities when they arrive.

Proverbs 1:5 reads:

The wise also will hear and increase learning, and the person of understanding

will acquire skill *and* attain to sound counsel [so that he may be able to steer his course rightly]. (AMP)

Never mind negative comments from a co-worker. *"You let the boss talk you into working overtime? Not me! I work five days a week. I need my Saturdays off!"* Those words are nothing more than cleverly disguised thoughts planted by the enemy. He sent that person to your desk with the intentions to cause you to second guess yourself. Can't you see what's happening? The enemy wants you to miss a God-appointed opportunity. Girlfriend, you'd better recognize! And, would you please stop listening to other people's garbage! Your supervisor could very well be setting you up for a promotion in the near future. Beware how people express their unsolicited opinions, or advice. I've come to learn in my good fight of faith, the more determined I am to possess what God says is available to me, the more I'm challenged to defend the faith I have in Him to make impossibilities into possibilities. Where do you think resistance comes from? Who wants to see you fail? Who'd rather see you go on living paycheck-to-paycheck? Need I say more?

When people realize I'm a woman not easily swayed by what falls out of their mouths, they approach me differently from everybody else. That's not a bad thing. It lets them know they cannot step to me talking any ole' trash. It also blocks distraction. If I'm not preoccupied, lingering over what *they* said,

Go Beyond Your Dreams
(Live Them!)

I'm more receptive to what the Holy Spirit has to say to me. What He has to say to me is more important than anything someone else might have to say about my prosperity. At least I know He's on my side!

Reprogram your mind to listen for His quiet, still voice for direction—which could come at any given moment. *"Do it this way."* Move! Do what He tells you! If you're not quite sure if what you heard was really direction from the Holy Spirit, ask Him. "Was that you?"

James 1:5 reads:

> **If any of you is deficient in wisdom, let him ask of the giving God [Who gives] to everyone liberally *and* ungrudgingly, without reproaching *or* faultfinding, and it will be given to him.** (AMP)

Wouldn't it be better to consult God rather than keep silent wondering, possibly letting a great opportunity slip through your fingers? To do nothing could prove to be a grave error on your part. It also might be a while before another opportunity like that comes around again because you failed to recognize it was God making it available for you. Remember Sarah? She didn't bother to ask, "Lord is that You?" Instead she chuckled to herself listening to the voice in her head and not her heart. Sarah concluded within herself, (in my own words), "there is no way getting pregnant a possibility!"

Girlfriend, show God you're trustworthy with His visions and dreams for you. Then stand back! Brace yourself! Begin expecting situations to change for the better in your favor. If God be for you, who can be against you? When God looks upon the heart (faith) set on doing things His way, opportunities will rain down from heaven! Let it rain! Let it rain!

Deuteronomy 28:12 reads:

> **The Lord shall open to you His good treasury, the heavens, to give the rain of your land in its season and to bless all the work of your hands; and you shall lend to many nations, but you shall not borrow. (AMP)**

Our Heavenly Father will open doors for us that those in authoritative positions will no longer be able to shut in our face. Faith is an action word. The decision to step out of your comfort zone is a declaration. *"Here I am God! I'm ready to do what I'm equipped to do in the natural to the best of my knowledge. I'm trusting you, Lord for strength, wisdom and direction! You can trust me! I'm going to do this Your way!"*

Normally, when I think of the word *trust*, I'm drawn to largely consider an individual's character. I also factor in the integrity (or lack thereof), of their characteristics. Trust isn't something I take lightly. Therefore, I'm left to ask myself a few questions before breaching any confidentially. Has this person earned my trust? Have they proven they can reframe from divulging a confidence? What measure do they place on trust between themselves and others? For me, these are important questions to consider, especially if you see yourself as someone who is trustworthy. Why would we want to risk our integrity by becoming entangled with someone who doesn't share the same views as we do when it comes to genuine trust?

While my publisher Kathy and I were working on the final stages of this book she highlighted this subject—trust. Throughout the chapter I mentioned how important it was for God to be able to trust us with a dream or vision that we had received from Him. Kathy wanted me to go a little deeper. No problem. I could do that, not only because she's my publisher, but because our relationship is young. It is still being established. I did this because I want to *earn Kathy's trust*. She and I are in the process of 'getting to know one another.' What we learn from each other—about one another through the publishing of this book will determine how far our author/publisher working relationship progresses in the future. This means our professional and personal level of trust must exist between the two of us.

As usual, I turned to my *Strong's Concordance* for guidance to find scriptures relating to the word *trust*. I've always believed that while God speaks of being a God in whom we can trust, I felt it was as equally as important that we must be children He can trust also. After searching for the appropriate scriptures, I began reading the list I'd written down. Out of all the scriptures that I read in the Bible, two scriptures in Psalms 56 and 62 stirred my heart in a new way—a different way. It was like reading these verses for the first time. That's what I love about reading the Bible. I can read a scripture over and over again, but at a particular moment, during a particular need, a verse and/or verses can reveal a fresh interpretation meant to be revealed in a new way. Girlfriend, if I may, I'd like to share what **Psalms 56:11 and 62:8 reads:**

> **In God have I put my trust and confident reliance; I will not be afraid. What can man do to me?**
>
> **Trust in, lean on, rely on, *and* have confidence in Him at all times, you people; pour out your heart before Him. God is a refuge for us (a fortress and a high tower). (AMP)**

My understanding of these two scriptures became somewhat even clearer. How God feels about us being trustworthy closely resembles possessing hearts of faith. I felt these scriptures were telling me if we want to prove ourselves as women who God can trust, there are certain things we must attend to. First we have to build our hearts up on our strongest faith. Then we must wait (rest) in the faithfulness of God. However, while we're waiting it would serve us well to activate our faith by expecting. God is the

Go Beyond Your Dreams
(Live Them!)

stability we need in pursuit of our dreams. He alone will defend us against the naysayers when *they* say our dream(s) will never come to pass. We should show God how much we trust His Word by not allowing ourselves to be moved by what *they* say!

We can boldly stand with our heads held high, strengthened spiritually and mentally. God is a loving Father. He is compassionate, merciful, and discreet. In other words, anything we speak out of our hearts to our Heavenly Father will be our best guarded conversation. We can demonstrate trust by opening our hearts to God everyday—in everything!

God's Word emphatically states that we cannot please Him without faith. As a matter of fact, the scripture reads *it is impossible to please Him*. Faith is believing that He is able to do beyond anything we could ever begin to ask, or think. That involves trust! Therefore, we not only must please our Father walking by faith, I believe we must also please Him by exhibiting acts of committed trust. God's dreams (for us) are implanted inside of us long before we came into the earth.

Each day we spend walking by faith and not by sight, is another day to earn the complete trust of God. We must develop mindsets to become women who God trusts to walk unafraid to receive His goodness. Girlfriend, expose yourself to Him! It doesn't matter how your trust and faith may appear to others. So what! Do not be moved! Show God you understand what it means to be trustworthy by remaining in unwavering faith. Meanwhile as we wait expecting God to bring our dreams to fruition, remember He too is expecting something from us. He's expecting us to trust Him enough to manifest those dreams. Both faith and trust require making a commitment. God has already committed Himself by giving us His trustworthy, infallible Word!

CHAPTER 9
WHAT'S INSIDE YOUR HEART

The upright (honorable, intrinsically good) man out of the good treasure [stored] in his heart produces what is upright (honorable and intrinsically good), and the evil man out of the evil storehouse brings forth that which is depraved (wicked and intrinsically evil); for out of the abundance (overflow) of the heart his mouth speaks. (AMP)

Luke 6:45

One of the most important keys to unlocking faith is a heart of righteousness. It's imperative the reading of God's Word not be omitted from your spiritual exercises. The Word stimulates the heart to be receptive for increasing our level of faith. However, understand faith comes under scrutiny when others notice you don't quite fit the norm. So what! Discretion shows maturity and wisdom. God says you're a peculiar treasure unto Him. That means your actions concerning your personal welfare should be as individual as you are. You can only be good at being you. Taking on the characteristics of another person will rob the real you. Don't pretend to be anyone or anything other than who God created you to be. You're an original. Walk boldly, confident in who you are!

Personally, I don't have any problem standing out from my co-workers, or anyone else for that matter. I'm not anti-sociable, but I don't participate in all of the office activities either. There are a few women who I suspect are office gossips. I'm aware of this, so I'm cordial. But I keep my distance. As far as what happens in my personal life outside the office *they* are clueless. That's the way it should be. Women must learn to separate work associations from what goes on in their personal lives. One really has little to do with the other. Don't fall into the ole' cliché "we're one big happy family!" No. Co-workers aren't family. You have a family outside your work environment. Well, enough about that. I think you get the picture. It's okay to be a woman following after her heart, instead of being lead around by her head.

The bottom line is, people are always going to look at the outward appearance. That's just the way human beings are. For example. You work along side of another female you seldom, if ever hear her say an unkind word about anyone. She readily makes herself accessible whenever someone needs assistance in the office. She's always pleasant. You've never seen a day pass where she hasn't been friendly. This woman is generally thought of as a person with a kind heart—a good heart. But what her fellow co-workers don't see is that this same woman takes advantage of peak times in the office gossiping on the phone with her girlfriends about her family, the folks at church, and them too. Her co-workers don't have a clue while

Go Beyond Your Dreams
(Live Them!)

she's smiling, volunteering her help. She's really thinking, "why are they always bothering me?" Outside the office at home behind closed doors, this woman creates a hostile environment. She constantly screams, yells and curses at her husband and three kids. The outward appearance can be quite deceptive.

The heart of a woman is where it counts with God. He keenly observes the motivation in our hearts that push us to do what we do. God searches deep into the hidden agenda of our hearts. (I Sam. 16:7) (I Chr. 28:9) The truth is, God could care less about our cute dresses, handbags and matching platform shoes. He's more interested in how we maintain our heart. Girlfriend, it's a smart thing to re-evaluate the premise of our hearts on a regular basis. Honestly ask yourself. *"Have I allowed my heart to become polluted with ulterior motives?"* One thing we don't want to do is deceive ourselves. God searches for a pure heart. So before we go to God with our wish-list, we'd be wise to check the status of our heart. If it's not up-to-par at that particular moment, do the necessary aerobics to get your heart back in shape. God's Word shields us against our hearts becoming clogged with a lot of junk.

I know you've experienced this next scenario. Sista Gurl is eyeballing you up and down at church (you know that look). She gives you a phony hug, then whispers, *"you must buy new clothes every week."* Oh! No she didn't! What do you wanna bet Sista Gurl is envious of your wardrobe! Girlfriend, we both know it's a female thing to be catty with other females. *"Meow!"* Hard as it might be sometimes, we must be mindful to keep a clean, honest heart before the Lord. We don't want to run the risk of hindering our prayers by letting the actions and words of another move us. Take my advice. Flash Sista Gurl a big smile. Turn and walk away. Quick! Girlfriend, what lays up on the heart is eventually verbalized, whether it's spoken in a positive way, or uttered negatively. *"I can't stand her!"* (Lk. 6:45) We cannot go around thinking and talking like the world. Negative speech interferes with answered prayer. *"I hope I get it. Well, if it's meant to be, it'll happen. Seeing is believing. If I'm lucky. I wish."* And so on. Am I the only one who's unconsciously mumbled words like that? Come on girlfriend, you have too. Let's keep it real! Okay? You kid yourself if you think God isn't listening. It's only natural we might slip up here and there. God certainly knows we're not perfect. No one is, except our Heavenly Father. Therefore, imperfections abound. A conscientious decision to deposit God's Word into your heart has to become an attitude. It's an absolute to ward off saying dumb things. It's a required necessary nourishment for strengthening faith. Much in the same way we need vitamin supplements for maintaining healthy bodies, is the same way we need God's Word to keep our spirit healthy.

Go Beyond Your Dreams
(Live Them!)

Psalms 27:14 reads:

> **Wait and hope for and expect the Lord; be brave and of good courage and let your heart be stout and enduring. Yes, wait for and hope and expect the Lord. (AMP)**

The enemy doesn't like to see you living by faith (trusting in God's Word). He knows just how far an act of faith can take you. He's afraid if you know what he knows, he won't have a leg to stand on. Girlfriend, I say knock his legs right out from under him! Do your spiritual aerobic exercises everyday to strengthen your heart in God's Word. (Ps. 37:31) Here's another 'but' clause. But be crystal clear what's inside your heart before going to God in prayer. You don't want to ask Him to bless you with a new fancy red convertible sports car just because your neighbor across the street recently bought one. A jealous (covetous) heart isn't going to get you anything. Can't you be happy for your neighbor's good fortune? God will know which prayers come from a heart of envy, and prayers stimulated by a sincere need. He's an Omniscient God. There are no best kept secrets of the heart. He has the divine ability to look beyond our hearts to see the true motives behind our prayers. (Ps. 90:8) (Mk. 4:22) (Lk. 8:17)

Ecclesiastes 12:14 reads:

For God shall bring every work into judgment, with every secret thing, whether it is good or evil. (AMP)

Similarities between the tongue and the heart make both of them susceptible to corruption. You'd be surprised to know how many undetected influences from others play a significant role in keeping our faith. I've read the scripture in II Corinthians that pertains to being unequally yoked over a dozen times, or more. I thought it referred to Christians marrying non-believers. (II Cor. 6:15) However, while writing this book I read it again. This time I interpreted this scripture in a new light. That verse could just as easily be interpreted as Christians straddling the fence. Let me explain myself. There's a sentence in that scripture which raises the question. *"What has a believer in common with an unbeliever?"* I read it in relation to the kinds of friendships and associations we form. Another passage of scripture also came to mind.

I Peter 1:23 reads:

You have been regenerated (born again), not from a mortal origin (seed sperm), but from one that is immortal by the ever living and lasting Word of God. (AMP)

Go Beyond Your Dreams
(Live Them!)

Can you think of a better way to get you to take your eyes off God, than through the negative suggestions or ideas planted by someone who doesn't practice living by faith? The fact is, the enemy roams about trying to see who he can destroy. (I Pet. 5:8) The enemy devises schemes by any means necessary to tear down a Christian woman's faith. He will purposely use unsuspecting people who are closest to us. The enemy knows that if he doesn't cripple our faith, dreams will become a reality. He doesn't want us to give God the glory for anything! The enemy works against us! He goes into action using the mind and mouth of a faith-buster. His strategy deliberately takes aim to get you off course. He hopes if you hear enough objective views, you'll begin to doubt God, and soon after doubt yourself. If he succeeds in his plan, there's every chance of you growing weak in your heart, and walking away from achieving prosperity. You'll stop believing that it's possible. You'll stop trusting God at His Word.

Girlfriend, we're dealing with a clever, lying devil. We have to be smarter than he is! Don't jeopardize what God says you can have. Whenever you accept the advice (counsel) of someone who doesn't acknowledge God, you play a risky game. You could find yourself slowing down in your daily spiritual aerobics. You become lazy about praying. The pages of your Bible go unopened for days. You start to wonder if perhaps the person who gave you that frivolous advice could possibly be right. Doubt creeps in clouding your better judgment. Then that nagging question settles in. *"What if?"* Meanwhile, the ungodly counsel you received (in your spirit), has corrupted your heart. Faith no longer has residence. That's why it's very important we continuously pray to receive a discerning spirit. We want to be able to instantly detect schemes and trickery of the adversary with spiritual eyes and spiritual ears when he comes lurking around us.

The Word of God can be used as a weapon against deception. However, unless you know, that you know, the enemy can easily put one over on you. Girlfriend, all that glitters isn't gold! From time to time you may need to ask yourself. *"How does this person, or persons define me in correlation to my dreams?"* If all you've ever heard fall out of their mouth are words of skepticism and pessimism, how can *they* possibly be in agreement with you? The hearts and minds of others aren't necessarily in sync with where you're coming from. You want to become skillful in discerning slick individuals speaking out of calculating hearts. *"That sounds like a great idea! But are you sure you wanna quit your job to do that?"* More than likely they can't wait to disclose the conversation about your vision to others. *"I bet you'd be good at doing that!"* They grin. *"Aren't you scared that you might not get a loan from the bank?"* Then here comes a sly maneuver. *"Gotta go!"*

No sooner than your back is turned, that person is conspiring (gossiping) about your personal business, hoping to see you fail! She tells somebody. They tell somebody. And, all parties involved make you the talk of their conversations. While you shared a part of yourself out of an honest heart, your friend's heart was in another place. Don't put yourself in a position to fall victim to what you see (natural eyes) on the outside. There are many beautiful (physical beauty), conniving, back-stabbing, and manipulative people in the world. The enemy will send them directly to you. Petition God to give you spiritual sight, along with a discerning spirit. The enemy purposely comes to steal God's Word out of the hearts of women who strongly believe their dreams are possible. He'll have seemingly trusting people (on the surface) approach you out of nowhere. He'll send ones who irritate you the most at your job to casually drop by your desk. And, let's not forget the people who say all the nice things they think you want to hear, only to try to get you to divulge juicy details about yourself.

Matthew 12:34-35 reads:

> **You offspring of vipers! How can you speak good things when you are evil (wicked)? For out of the fullness (the overflow, the superabundance) of the heart the mouth speaks. The good man from his inner good treasure flings forth good things, and the evil man out of his inner evil storehouse flings forth evil things. (AMP)**

Another deception we probably think little of is misinterpreting the increase of things as a definition for success. Gawking too closely at the good fortune of someone else opens the door to covetousness. You'll be so busy keeping tabs on their goods, you may not perceive your heart is filling itself with strife. Envy and jealousy have one function. They produce discord. Faith can't survive. It will not remain when you let the wrong things in.

Upon accepting Jesus into our hearts, we become born-again spiritually. As born-again Christian women we go from being poor lost souls, to becoming heirs, saved by the blood of Jesus! God's Word says we're eligible to possess all things! There's no need for any of us to be envious of one another! Be mindful. Keep guard over your heart.

Now, if you think of yourself as a spiritually strong woman, don't pat yourself on the back. The only reason why you haven't lost your mind is because God is keeping you. His loving-kindness and tender mercies are new every morning. It's by His grace that we're able to withstand (persevere) life's problems. God is a compassionate Father. He loves you! He understands His daughters probably better than we understand ourselves the majority of time.

Lamentations 3:22-26 reads:

> **It is because of the Lord's mercy and loving-kindness that we are not consumed, because His [tender]**

compassion fail not, they are new every morning; great and abundant is Your stability and faithfulness. The Lord is my portion or share, says my living being (my inner self); therefore will I hope in Him and wait expectantly for Him. The Lord is good to those who wait hopefully and expectantly for Him, to those who seek Him [inquire of and for Him and require Him by right necessity and on the authority of God's Word]. It is good that one should hope in and wait quietly for the salvation (the safety and ease of the Lord) (AMP)

You want to know something? It's not whether we can trust God. But rather, can He trust us? Will we be good and faithful stewards with His visions for us? God carefully studies the heart. He searches for hidden agendas, or selfish motives. (Prov. 21:2) It doesn't matter how much we pray, or believe. If our heart isn't in line with God's Word, it will take longer for dreams to come to pass. God wants to be certain He can trust us with the small blessings before He promotes us to larger ones.

Exercise your heart to increase your level of trust in God. Wait quietly for His direction. Stop agreeing with folks who smile in your face, then tell all your business behind your back! Stay true to yourself. Don't compromise faith by running your mouth to people who do not have your best interest at heart. Over the years, I've learned by consistently doing spiritual aerobics to strengthen my heart in God's Word, faith definitely increases. You mustn't become easily distracted by what you hear, and even less by what you see. A committed heart of faith deeply rooted and grounded in God's Word is a heart that releases dreams. Girlfriend, trust God that your visions, dreams, and ideas in the spirit realm will come to fruition when your heart lines up with what He says is available to you!

CHAPTER 10
PEACE OF MIND IS A NECESSITY

I will listen [with expectancy] to what God the Lord will say, for He will speak peace to His people, to His saints (those who are in right standing with Him)—but let them not turn again to [self-confident] folly. (AMP)

Psalms 85:8

While in pursuit of your vision and/or dream, not only is it important that you function with a sound mind, but it's equally as important to operate with peace of mind. Grant you, there will be distractions. However, negative disruptions in your thought process only occur to thwart confusion.

James 1:2-4 reads:

> **Consider it a sheer gift, friends, when tests and challenges come at you from all sides. You know that under pressure, your faith-life is forced into the open and shows its true colors. So don't try to get out of anything prematurely. Let it do its work so you become mature and well-developed, not deficient in any way.** (THE MESSAGE)

Remember you're never without help. (Ps. 121:2) We have a promise that if we keep our eyes focused on God; He will keep us in perfect peace. (Isa. 26:3) Despite the fact you can't see (with the natural eyes) your desire as a reality today, doesn't mean you won't begin to see it (through spiritual eyes) tomorrow, or the day after that. A woman of mature faith doesn't readily accept what she sees. Instead, she lives by heart-filled faith, trusting God all the way.

Lamentations 3:37 reads:

Who is he who speaks and it comes to pass, if the Lord has not authorized *and* commanded it? (AMP)

As I mentioned previously, this may not be the right, or appropriate time to share what God has given you. You could be asking for trouble, if you do. Consider this scenario for a moment. We'll call this woman Lilly. She happily expresses an idea she has to a friend at church who she's known for years. The one person Lilly thought would be happy for her doesn't have one positive word to say. Instead of encouraging Lilly, church lady doesn't blink as she responds. *"That's a dumb idea! Why would you want to waste your time doing that? Surely, nothing can come of it!"* The only thing Lilly can do is return a blank stare. She's dumbfounded, unable to believe what she just heard. It's not church lady's fault for reacting that way. She believes it's okay to be content

Go Beyond Your Dreams
(Live Them!)

with what she already has (or doesn't have) from a materialistic standpoint. Somewhere in the back of church lady's mind, she's convinced herself if she doesn't desire anything she can't be disappointed trying to achieve something she doesn't really believe could ever happen anyway.

Too many women feel, and think defeat without ever have given themselves a fighting chance. Sadly, this is where second guessing, fueled by influences of someone else could come into play. God's Word is simple. Do not let another person rationalize your ideas for successful living! God is well able to give us above and beyond anything we could ever ask or think! Girlfriend, now I ask you. Doesn't that sound like God wants us to dream, and dream big?

Ephesians 3:20 reads:

> **God can do anything, you know—far more than you could ever imagine or guess or request in your wildest dreams!** (THE MESSAGE)

It finally hit me during my separation. It's not *what we know* that frightens us. It's *what we don't know* that keeps us living paycheck-to-paycheck. Many of us run out of money before the end of the month. I can only speak for myself, but I'm really, really, really tired of having more month left over than money! The enemy is slick. He knows exactly how to steal a woman's peace. He goes right for the jugular. He attacks our pocketbooks! You'd think he'd know better than to mess with a woman and her money! And, why must it always be on Mondays when the enemy starts stealing out of my wallet?

Money is a necessity for practically everything. Who doesn't know that? But did you know scarceness, barrenness or the constant lack of it can steal our peace? We start worrying how we're going to pay for this, and pay for that. It's very difficult to consider pursuing a dream once worry sets in. I know what I'm talking about. Writing quickly becomes the furthest thing from my mind. I'm too busy worrying if I can pay all of my bills, or at least pay them on time when a lack-attack comes along.

Fear and worry are just two strategies the enemy uses to ambush peace. He unleashes restlessness (not sure what to do), confusion (should I?), procrastination (I'll do it later), and strife (easily agitated). Negative emotions combined with foggy thoughts are spiritual attacks. The enemy is trying to throw a monkey wrench into your dreams. He'll do anything to slow down your progress. He knows once you're distracted by one thing after another, you won't devote much time to launching a plan into action. That's precisely what the enemy is banking on. The minute our mind starts to focus more on our problems, we're liable to push a dream so far back, eventually we block it out completely. Suddenly the problem becomes more important. Girlfriend, recognize the enemy for who he is. A liar! The

Go Beyond Your Dreams
(Live Them!)

enemy wears many masks. Have you ever heard that old phrase, *"smiling faces tell lies?"*

How many dreamers reading this book are discouraged from working for someone else? On top of feeling this way are you desiring to do what seems impossible? Out of discouragement are your dreams becoming lost in the shuffle of life? I wouldn't be at all surprised if most women lose interest in pursuing a dream because they no longer have peace. I've been there myself. We all need our jobs. I'm not saying quit. What I'm trying to say is this. Work to pay the bills, but don't let having a job stop you from pursuing your visions and dreams to believe doing what you love to do. I say all the time that my job is my hobby, and writing is my work. Writing is where I find fulfillment. This is what I love to do. Don't let circumstances take precedence over following your hearts desire. I've been there—done that.

Girlfriend, can we get one thing clear? God doesn't only give men visions and dreams for witty inventions; He also imparts creative ideas into women. God is no respecter of persons. Men aren't the only ones who have what it takes to conquer new pursuits. God takes pleasure in His daughters living out their divine purposes, which have specifically been designed for each individual female.

There's another way to lose peace. It's by allowing yourself to succumb to envious tendencies. What God has for you is for you only. What He has for another woman is just for her. Unlike mankind, God doesn't exhibit impartiality.

Acts 10:34 reads:

> **And Peter opened his mouth and said: Most certainly *and* thoroughly I now perceive *and* understand that God shows no partiality *and* is no respecter of persons.** (AMP)

For one moment, I'd like to tie in another area where women lose their peace. At fifty-something, I'm going through menopause. However, I'm not insensitive to the women who still have menstrual cycles. I remember that particular time of the month, which brings me to my point. When you start acting bizarre, that's probably a good time to zero in on what's actually happening to you. Every month women find themselves irritable, mean-spirited, touchy-feely, quick tempered, and downright miserable for no apparent reason. The medical society legalized those emotions. We now know it's perfectly alright to lose our minds one week out of each month. Well, you know what? Peace goes on hiatus during that certain time of the month.

Girlfriend, take a deep breath. Grab your Bible. Renew your mind. God's Word not only replenishes our spirit, but it can restore peace to our mind. Couldn't you use some peace during those particular days? Especially on those days?

Go Beyond Your Dreams
(Live Them!)

Psalms 29:11 reads:

The Lord will give [unyielding and impenetrable] strength to His people; the Lord will bless His people with peace. (AMP)

We have the promise of God to bless us with peace. Prosperity depends heavily on the state of your mind. Permit your Heavenly Father to guide you every step of the way. There's one other thing worth mentioning here. Turning a deaf ear to others from time to time can be a good thing. The only voice we need to adhere to is the voice of our Heavenly Father. He'll always know what's best for us. Remember, words have a way of performing two things: (1) positive reactions, or (2) negative reactions.

Unfortunately, when it comes to pursuing a prosperous lifestyle, people seldom offer words of encouragement. You can usually count on them having plenty of negative words to shower on you. The bottom line is this. Attitudes, opinions, and negative logistics from people chip away at our peace. There's an old saying, *"The world didn't give it to me, and the world can't take it away."* That phrase is actually referring to joy, but it could just as easily refer to peace. Once you've made the quality decision to seriously achieve your dream, don't let anyone, or anything steal your peace during the process.

While traveling along the road to prosperity, you're probably going to hit a snag or two, or three. But what should it matter? Adversity makes you stronger. First and foremost, remember who you are! Brush yourself off. Then get back on the path God has chosen for your feet to tread. He's already walked out your steps. You only need to follow behind Him.

Proverbs 20:24 reads:

The very steps we take come from God; otherwise how would we know where we're going? (THE MESSAGE)

God knew the precise moment when this journey of ours would begin. He knows the exact minute it will end. Although I suspect I might ruffle a few feathers, this is an honest observation. Females can be some of the most envious, the most jealous, petty creatures God ever created. And, to every female reading this book, I said this in love. Girlfriend, if your desire is to live beyond your dreams, then you'd best not be led by the above mentioned negatives. There's little room for peace when a heart is motivated by ugly emotions. Anything worth having doesn't happen without concessions. Weigh the pros and cons. Balance out what's beneficial and what's not, according to where you see yourself going. For instance, you've told yourself within the next two years you want to open a catering business. However, you continue to put the

Go Beyond Your Dreams
(Live Them!)

needs of others ahead of your own. That's improper balance. To be in a position where someone else wants and needs are more important than your own is out of order. Girlfriend, the word "no" can be a good thing. I've learned making sacrifices also involves temporarily stepping away from the girlfriend circuit. It may be somewhat rough at first when you have to turn down a Saturday afternoon shopping trip to the mall with the girls. More than likely it won't be any easier saying no to Sunday brunch either, but you're stronger than you think. You might experience a tingling in your ears when it comes time to shorten those phone sessions. The way I see it, a conversation between two women past an hour isn't a phone call, it's a phone drama session. You might have to pass on the after work Friday girl's night out to eat dinner and see a movie. Try looking at it this way. You'll save $10.00 for a movie ticket. Within a few months the movie will probably be on DVD anyway. Girlfriend, a dream demands your undivided attention. If you must watch current movies, buy yourself a microwave. Pick up some microwave popcorn at the grocery store. Then become a member at your neighborhood video rental store!

  All kidding aside (I'm laughing). Haven't you waited long enough for change? Well, if change is what you want, there will be friends who are going to see less of you. If you're working hard at perfecting your craft as best you can, they'll probably hear even less from you. The bottom line is this. If those same friends are still around when you start enjoying the benefits of a few sacrifices, they were loyal friends. However, during your absence if you've been replaced by a new face ... need I say more? I'm learning ways that lead to a loss of peace actually aren't that obvious. The lack of peace easily goes undetected. Let me give you a for instance.

In the early stages of a brilliant idea (everything begins with a thought) a woman I'll call Helen, is thrilled she's going back to college to pursue her Masters Degree. Following a lengthy conversation with her spouse, they both agree the kids are old enough now where she could go back to school at night. Her husband offers to help with their 10 year old twins in between his hectic work schedule. Two weeks later while Helen is standing in line to register for classes her mind races back to a recent conversation with her sister. Without realizing it, Helen no longer has peace while standing in line.

Since talking to her sister, Helen has developed an unrest in her spirit. She began second guessing her decision to go to school. Helen's sister was happy when she talked about her plans to get her degree. Her sister volunteered to watch the twins in the evenings and help out as much as she possibly could. With all this support being offered to assist Helen in achieving her dream, the enemy planted doubt inside Helen's head. *"At age 48, aren't you too old to be thinking about getting your degree? You're only kidding yourself thinking you can do it all. What*

Go Beyond Your Dreams
(Live Them!)

about trying to keep up with homework assignments? What if your family needs your attention, and you're too busy with night school to notice? What if?"

The second Helen made a decision to do things God's way, the enemy immediately attacked her mind. He wanted to destroy her vision, kill any ideas she might have in between, and steal the dream of receiving her Master's Degree. Meanwhile, during the 40 minute drive from the college campus to home, Helen felt confused. Suddenly she questioned whether she was doing the right thing. By the time she reached the driveway of her home, Helen was strongly considering putting off college for another year. At least if she waited, the twins would be a year older. Perhaps if she waited, it would be better for her, and her family. She hadn't gone back to school in all this time, what difference was another year going to make?

Helen is fiction, but the story is very real. How many times have we changed our minds about something that possibly would've moved us closer to achieving the desires of our heart? If the enemy can accomplish keeping us right where we are, success will always elude us. Therefore, it's imperative for us to be on spiritual guard at all times. Even when things are going good in our lives we can't let our guard down a tiny bit, WE CAN'T! The enemy roams about seeing who he can destroy. (I Pet. 5:8) If we drop our guard, we open ourselves up for a sneak attack. He sends doubt to our thought process in an attempt to disrupt our peace of mind. Confusion mixed with doubt interferes with peace. Irrational behavior transforms an otherwise peaceful woman into a woman of indecisiveness.

Negative emotions raise their ugly heads creating spiritual chaos. Unrest, tension, irritability, contention, easily offended, argumentative, and worrying every five minutes over nothing are indicators (red flags) you don't have inner peace. Jesus said, *"Be anxious for nothing!"* The enemy notices how excited we are about our future. He sees us resting in the peace of God. He sees how much we are increasing our faith to have whatsoever we desire. The enemy watches how much our faith matures, trusting God at His Word. This is too much for the devil. He gets scared. So he deliberately flips our inner peace upside down. This is the same devil who tricked God's first woman (Eve). The devil hates women! He still tries to trick us today! Prosperity (God's way) isn't what the enemy wants for you. He hates to see any woman prospering in the goodness of God! The enemy would rather strip females spiritually powerless and have us living in poverty. He doesn't want us to trust God, or believe in any of God's promises.

Throughout the course of chasing dreams, the enemy is going to pull sneak attacks. Suddenly people start dropping by your house unannounced interrupting you from what you need to be doing. Sometimes the enemy will even kick it up a notch.

Go Beyond Your Dreams
(Live Them!)

The phone starts ringing off the hook. People you haven't talked to in months are now calling. Then finally, the enemy goes full force! He plants negative words in the mouth of someone closest to you. This person has been sent on an unsuspecting assignment to deliberately take the wind out of your sails. In the meantime, the enemy is sitting back waiting, hoping you took the bait. He's watching, studying your actions very closely.

But wait a minute! Somebody push rewind! Who does this vision belong to? Did God give it to family? Friends? No! He gave it to you! Girlfriend, please skill yourself in recognizing negative set-ups (fiery darts) to discourage you from taking possession of your destiny! The enemy uses sly, slick, and wicked approaches meant to snip away at peace. As heirs to the Kingdom, we can qualify ourselves to experience sweat-less victories!

I Corinthians 15:57-58 reads:

> **But thanks be to God, Who gives us the victory [making us conquerors] through our Lord Jesus Christ. Therefore, my beloved brethren be firm (steadfast), immovable, always abounding in the work of the Lord [always being superior, excelling, doing more than enough in the service of the Lord], knowing *and* being continually aware that your labor in**

the Lord is not futile [it is never wasted or to no purpose]. (AMP)

Girlfriend, anything God has placed His hands upon runs smoothly. (Lk. 3:5) However, you should also be aware that while that's true, adversity is sure to stir things up a bit. Adversity comes to keep you from moving ahead. Girlfriend, don't be swayed by distractions. Whenever you start feeling anxious, ask God to cover you with *His kind of peace* that is able to supersede all of your understanding. In other words, when all hell is breaking loose around you, there'll be peace in your spirit, soul, mind, and body in spite of it. (Phil. 4:7; 4:9) (Col. 3:15) You'll be as cool as a cucumber. Your actions may be confusing to everybody else, but God said He'd confound the wise. (I Cor. 1:27)

I'd like for you to picture this for a minute. There's another woman experiencing the same type of problem you're facing right now. The difference between the two of you is, she has decided to give up. This woman has allowed the enemy to fill her head with bees. You on the other hand have diligently been exercising your faith day after day. Following weeks of spiritual aerobics, the strategies the enemy tried to use against you no longer get past the guard (God's Word) you've placed around your mind. You won't let his devilish ploys penetrate your peace. You know who you are. You refuse to give up on God, His Word, the Holy Spirit or yourself. Do you know what's happening? You've learned how to exercise your spiritual aerobics as a part of your everyday life!

Aren't you tired of being pregnant with a vision? Isn't it time you took it seriously? Don't you want to give birth to this dream you've been carrying around for so long? Aren't you ready to go into labor to push forth your God-ordained prosperity? Can't you see yourself in the vision living out your dreams? Did you get tingly inside when you saw God's vision for your future? Then you must stop letting the enemy, and his home boys deceive you! We can't be afraid to become dream chasers! We've got to develop confidence with the clear understanding that no weapon (crisis) formed (attack) against (carried out) us will prosper!

Isaiah 54:17 reads:

> **But no weapon that is formed against you shall prosper, and every tongue that shall rise against you in judgment you shall show to be in the wrong. This [peace, righteousness, security, triumph over opposition] is the heritage of the servants of the Lord [those in whom the ideal Servant of the Lord is reproduced]; this is the righteousness *or* the vindication which they obtain from Me [this is that which I impart to them as their justification], says the Lord.** (AMP)

You and I are never alone, even during those moments when we experience loneliness in our pursuits. We feel like there isn't anyone who could possibly understand what we're going through. God made a promise to never leave our sides. (Heb. 13:5) So whenever your spirit tells you that peace is starting to slip away, call on God to help you get it back! Stay in the good fight of faith. I don't care how long it takes. Refuse to let go! Trust God!

The peace (no worry) of God will be your strength through every kind of situation. (Ps. 33:20; 40:17; 70:5) His kind of peace is a guarantee not to let us faint (grow weary in our minds) before His appointed purpose for us.

Psalms 46:1 reads:

> **God is our Refuge and Strength [mighty *and* impenetrable to temptation], a very present *and* well-proved help in trouble. (AMP)**

Girlfriend, work those spiritual muscles! Develop (increase) your faith. Believe (tenaciously) with all of your heart! Don't be swayed by what you see, or what you hear. A stable mind, operating out of a peaceful assured heart will lead to divine destiny. God has equipped you with the ability to command peace to dwell wherever you are, and whenever you need it. Peace is a vital necessity in following your heart (faith).

*Go Beyond Your Dreams
(Live Them!)*

CHAPTER 11
LIVE IN PEACE WITH YOUR PROSPERITY

> You will guard him *and* keep him in perfect *and* constant peace whose mind [both its inclination and its character] is stayed on You, because he commits himself to You, leans on You, *and* hopes confidently in You. (AMP)
>
> Isaiah 26:3

Girlfriend, will you permit yourself to believe with all of your heart that your dream is within reach? Can you actually see yourself living beyond your dream? Well, if you can believe and see (through spiritual eyes) yourself in this dream, you're half way there! Let me be the first to encourage you to stand your ground! Our God is able to make dreams possible! (Ps. 35:27)

In the Book of Mark, Jesus was asleep on a boat traveling with His disciples. All of a sudden, out of nowhere arose a severe storm. The disciples bodies were tossed around the boat like rag dolls. They feared for their lives. Out of the twelve frightened men, one went to wake Jesus. I'm not going to tell the entire story. Read it for yourself. There's nothing like reading the Word of God for oneself. (Neh. 8:8)

Meanwhile, the boat rocked savagely against the raging sea waters. The terror filled disciples looked on as Jesus took authority over the storm. ***"Peace be still!"*** Jesus rebuked those strong gusting winds and rough waters. Immediately, peace fell over the sea. Within seconds the wind ceased. The raging water calmed itself. Jesus spoke three words, and that storm obeyed. (Mk. 4:37-39) Jesus gave us an example to follow whenever we're confronted by sudden storms in our lives. We've been given the authority as adopted daughters—heirs to God's Kingdom, to speak to our situations. We can put a demand on peace to come to our rescue. At no time do we have to subject ourselves to anything or anyone disturbing our peace of mind. And frankly speaking, any unexpected storm (problem) is an interruption in your flow of peace.

Storms come to shake our faith. They arrive (stirred up by the enemy), to stop us from achieving what God has already determined He has for us. Sudden, fast moving storms come along to make us question faith. Doubtfulness ultimately will generate a spirit of fear. The lack of the God-kind of faith opens the door to fear. A faithless heart frets and worries over everything.

In times such as a difficult storm you shouldn't be idle doing nothing. Girlfriend, exercise your faith. Put one foot in front of the other, and start walking towards the problem. Scared or not, you have to get out of a sinking boat. Trust Jesus! Join Him on the water! Jesus won't let your feet slip out from under you! Peace can permeate every area of a turbulent situation. There isn't anyone who's going to believe in your dreams more than you will. No one can pray for them to manifest like you will. No one will ever have more faith in her heart for your dreams than you will. Know this, a God-given dream belongs to the dreamer. No one will see it (the vision) the way you do because it's yours, and yours alone.

Job 33:15 reads:

[One may hear God's voice] in a dream, in a vision of the night, when deep sleep falls on men while slumbering upon the bed, (AMP)

In the book of Daniel, he speaks of a God in Heaven who reveals secrets. As you're reading, the book of Daniel, you'll note he is referring to King Nebuchadnezzar's dreams and visions. Our God is no respecter of persons. Visions, dreams, and desires of the heart that seemingly come out of nowhere, come from God. And, in due time God begins to reveal glances into those visions and dreams that are coming to pass. The God, Daniel speaks of in Heaven is the same God we serve today. He never changes. (Dan. 2:28-29) God is the same today, tomorrow, and forever. People might tell you out of politeness they understand what you're seeing. But the truth is, they scarcely imagine what you've actually seen. It's not their vision. Therefore, how can you expect them to see it exactly as it was given to you?

Girlfriend, I said all of that to say this. You're under no obligation to share every intricate detail established between you and God. Why? Because not everyone has a desire to challenge themselves to fulfill dreams. Not everybody will want to lead an abundant, successful lifestyle. I know it's hard to believe, but there are people content to stay right where they are. And, if they're happy, I say leave them alone. Usually there's some type of fear preventing them from stepping away from familiarity. For them it's comfortable. They feel safe. Sadly, they dare not allow themselves to hope for anything beyond what they can see in front of them. After all, playing it safe eliminates pressure. Unfortunately, if people hear negative words spoken over them enough, fear and doubt trickle down to their heart.

You may not experience any raging storms in your life. If not, that's a good thing. However, don't count on it never happening. Be wise enough to know a storm or two, or three could flair up at almost any given time, on any given day. If peace isn't found resting in your spirit, soul, mind and body, how can you stay focused on important matters? You can't. You won't. A lack of peace prevents your heart from showing you (through spiritual eyes), the dream as clearly as it did before. Regrettably, when that happens you may still think about your dream on occasion, but you won't care to do much more than that. Girlfriend, that's a spirit of unrest that has taken up residence inside your heart. Serve notice of eviction! This is no time to feel sorry for yourself. You have to put a demand on peace! We have a promise from God that if we keep our mind on Him, He will give us perfect peace. (Isa. 26:3) Peace of spirit, mind, body and soul belongs to us. Delayed doesn't mean denied. And remember, if you allow your heart to become polluted by envy and jealousy, yet speak of having faith, you're only lying to yourself. The possession of these emotions is robbing your faith.

James 3:14 and 3:16 reads:

> **But if you have bitter jealousy (envy) and contention (rivalry, selfish ambition) in your hearts, do not pride yourselves on it and thus be in defiance of *and* false to the Truth. For wherever there is jealousy (envy) and contention (rivalry and selfish ambition), there will also be confusion (unrest, disharmony, rebellion) and all sorts of evil *and* vile practices. (AMP)**

These are reckless emotions which hinder us from receiving what God says is available. The full intent of the enemy's actions are to trick you. If he can convince you nothing is ever going to change, eventually you will grow weary. I've been there. I've done that. But the devil is a liar! Girlfriend, stay diligent in your aerobic exercises. Maintain a guard around your heart-filled faith, declaring God's Word with a mind that is at peace. Jesus died on the cross. God raised Him up so that we might have life more abundantly. Abundance here on earth. Abundance when we come to Heaven. Do you get it? An abundant lifestyle belongs to you! Don't let family, friends, or anyone else make you believe different. We're entitled to live out our dreams! It's our covenant right! We don't have to be afraid to reach high. And, whatever you do, mean what you say! (Jas. 3:18) The fact is, the enemy will use any means necessary to manipulate your mind and distort the truth. He tries turning the mind against the heart. Be forewarned.

Maintaining peace of mind is detrimental to your spirit. Possessing a heart of faith serves as a claim on the promises of God. A clear mind completely focused on what God says can't miss. (Prov. 16:9) However, you must be in a position to receive clarity from His voice of instruction.

I Peter 2:21 reads:

> **This is the kind of life you've been invited into, the kind of life Christ lived. He suffered everything that came his way so you would know that it could be done, and also know how to do it, step-by-step.** (THE MESSAGE)

Go Beyond Your Dreams
(Live Them!)

Clear, concise thinking helps to keep us from making hasty, irrational decisions. Guidance is easily perceived within our spirit because God's direction is simple to follow. He doesn't confuse you by making it complicated. There's an assurance of peace in preparation to do what God instructs.

I Corinthians 14:33 reads:

> **For He [Who is the source of their prophesying] is not a God of confusion *and* disorder but of peace *and* order. As [is the practice] in all the churches of the saints (God's people),** (AMP)

From time to time you may need to double up on an exercise to replenish your spirit. But don't forget to remind yourself—**IT'S ONLY A MATTER OF TIME BEFORE MY VISION IS COMING TO FRUITION!**

Habakkuk 2:3 reads:

> **For the vision is yet for an appointed time and it hastens to the end [fulfillment]; it will not deceive *or* disappoint. Though it tarry, wait [earnestly] for it, because it will surely come; it will not behindhand on its appointed day.** (AMP)

It's like I've been saying all along. Not everybody is going to want to throw you a ticker tape parade just because you have visions and dreams. Peace of mind is what's going to assist faith with accomplishment. The enemy wants you to think you're undeserving. He'd rather you believe you're not worthy of God's absolute best. Girlfriend, a confused mind will believe that nonsense. But a mind resting in God's perfect peace won't fall victim to such lies.

In times where I'm engaging in a positive conversation and it begins leaning toward unproductive speaking, I politely step back. There are dozens of people who look at the glass half empty. They're seldom happy about anything. Negative words generated by an unproductive attitude make me back off—quick! If there's one thing I've learned during my faith fight is how to distance myself from faith-busters. It's obvious to me, we're not on the same page. Apparently we stand on an extremely different level of faith. Please do not misunderstand what I'm saying. I am not speaking against the measure of another person's faith. As individuals, we each must draw our own conclusions of those we surround ourselves with.

I used to accept what other people spoke over me, and my future. I'd find myself agreeing with them. After reading what God says about me, I no longer allow others to spew whatever they feel like saying in my presence. As a child of God, I know I can do all things through Christ, who strengthens me spiritually and mentally. (Phil. 4:13)

Go Beyond Your Dreams
(Live Them!)

Are you serious about fulfilling the desires of your heart? Because if you are, then do yourself a huge favor by adopting the attitude of a faith warrior. A tenacious state of mind is going to be what sets you apart from everyone else. You and *only you* are responsible for achieving those visions and dreams. God pre-ordained a divine destiny for you long before you were born. Take it from me, His kind of peace has a way of sustaining you, regardless of what hurdles you face in life.

The closer you draw to reaching your level of prosperity, the enemy is going to try harder to create problems. Girlfriend, if you don't fight back, his strategies will steal your peace and joy. Remember, the plots of the enemy are intended to shake your faith. Let him know that he is messing with the wrong woman!

Tell the devil you're no longer going to take whatever he feels like dishing out. Let him know you won't give up! Girlfriend, plant your feet firmly on the ground, raise your fists, and prepare to take your peace back! Stay in the good fight of faith! In the future, when you're living out your dreams, you'll be so glad that you persevered under the pressure with a reinforced peace of mind.

Go Beyond Your Dreams
(Live Them!)

Go Beyond Your Dreams
(Live Them!)

CONCLUSION
GO BEYOND YOUR DREAMS!

It's my sincerest hope in some small way this book has encouraged a woman with God-given dreams to build her heart in faith. I pray you've been inspired to believe dreams really can come true when you permit God to be in control of the process. As a born-again Christian, I've matured in my faith enough to understand there is nothing I do in this earth that amounts to anything without including my Heavenly Father, Jesus Christ (the Anointed One), and the Holy Spirit. Everything that I set out to accomplish must involve them. Without the guidance of this dynamic, magnificent trio, I can do nothing. It doesn't matter what I may desire. The truth is, the Father, the Son, and the Holy Spirit are everything I need to fuel those dreams. I dare not exclude either one of them.

Girlfriend, to be quite frank, asking Jesus to come to live inside our heart is *very serious* business! Salvation is a life-saving decision. It's a decision between you and God. It's a decision that shouldn't be taken lightly. Salvation is a personal commitment to enter into a rewarding, intimate relationship with the Father.

For each woman who reads this book, I pray you'll take a different approach pursuing your dreams and visions. But more importantly, it's my prayer if you are not a born-again believer, that you'll make Jesus, Lord of your life by accepting that *He is the risen Christ!* Jesus died for our sins so that we might live (eternally) and have life (spiritually and naturally) more abundantly! All throughout the drafting of this book, it was my intention not to come off like a know-it-all because I still have so very far to go in my daily Christian walk.

I hope I was successful in exposing myself as a woman with flaws, and imperfections, yet comfortable being who I am. The reference to you as *girlfriend,* was my way of trying to connect one woman to another. It was meant to let you know I'm not a pretentious woman. I battle moments when I struggle with my faith. On occasion I experience bouts of laziness to follow through with doing my spiritual aerobic exercises. I like sitting on the couch (or in my bed) watching a movie as much as anyone else. I hope I made you laugh or chuckle while you were reading this book because laughter really is good for the soul.

More importantly, what I deeply, earnestly want to express one female to another is simply this. I'm human. I still have issues in certain areas where I need deliverance, which means I'm constantly in prayer asking God to fix things I'm unable to correct on my own. I'm a Christian, allowing God to use me as He will, and change everything about me that's not like Him.

I Corinthians 15:44 and 15:49 reads:

> **It is sown a natural body (physical); it is raised a supernatural (a spiritual) body. [As surely as] there is a physical body, and there is also a spiritual body. And just as we have borne the image [of the man] of dust, so shall we *and so let us* also bear the image [of the Man] of heaven. (AMP)**

Our Heavenly Father loves each and every one of His daughters. It's not God's Will that any of His children perish because they lack knowledge of the truth—the Gospel. Girlfriend, God doesn't care where we've been, or who we've been with. He doesn't care what we've done, or who we did it to. God no longer remembers our sins when we accept His Son, Jesus as our personal Lord and Savior. (Heb. 8:12) God understands the choices (the world v. Jesus) we make today could have a consequential effect where our spirit spends eternity. He quietly observes, hoping we'll rouse ourselves to wake up from deceived states of minds. He waits for us to realize He's always there. God desires that every one of His female creations would fully understand, with Him *all things are possible* for those who believe. That's where the widely referred term born-again believers stem from. Christians everywhere believe in the Trinity.

We humans like to think we're capable of fixing whatever needs to be fixed in our perplexed lives. Remember, earlier I wrote God looks into our hearts? Most humans are only able to grasp what is tangible. However, what might look good to you, isn't necessarily good for you. If it's from God, you won't be confused. You'll have peace. Your spirit will bear witness with the Holy Spirit. Perhaps you've been told God won't forgive you for past mistakes. Maybe you're thinking you're not worthy enough to have a dream come true. I'm here to tell you, those lies come straight from hell! God loves *all* of His daughters! According to His Word, not one of us is any good.

Psalms 14:2-3 and Romans 3:10 reads:

> **The Lord looked down from heaven upon the children of men to see if there were any who understood, dealt wisely,** *and* **sought after God, inquiring for** *and* **of Him** *and* **requiring Him [of vital necessity]. They are all gone aside, they have *all* together become filthy; there is none that does good** *or* **right, no not one. As it is written, None is righteous, just** *and* **truthful** *and* **upright** *and* **conscientious, no not one. (AMP)**

Go Beyond Your Dreams
(Live Them!)

So you see, without God's compassion and grace, none of us are any good. The Word of God tells me if any of us is good, it certainly isn't anything we've done of ourselves. It's by God's grace and mercy that we mature (spiritually) and develop (mentally) to blossom into virtuous women. The enemy would like nothing better than for all females (including me), with shaded pasts to believe God closes His ears when a *not-so-good* woman prays from a sincere heart. This deceptive lie keeps far too many young girls, and women from reaching out to the one man (the only man) who is able to save their very souls; Jesus Christ. He can dry your tears, carry you when you're too tired to go on, and show you a much better way to live.

Our Father is very concerned about what takes place in the lives of His daughters. God is a loving Father. He cares about you! You were fearfully and wonderfully made before conception occurred inside your mother's womb. (Isa. 44:2; 44:24) (Eph. 1:4) (Ps. 139:14) Stop letting the devil whisper a bunch of nonsense in your ears. He's a liar! From the moment we make our grand entrance into this world, God is already well informed what we'll do, and precisely the hour we're going to do it. There are no surprises with God!

Girlfriend, we might have a lot of dark secrets in our past that we wouldn't dare share with anyone. Some of us are carrying around a lot of emotional baggage from our past. Then there are some of us who are front'n. We're wearing big smiles for people, but deep down inside we're hurting because we can't let go of our past. We're lonely because of bad choices in past relationships. We're wondering why we can't get ahead, but fail to realize we keep looking back. We're single mothers raising children on our own. We're company executives and administrators who clawed our way to get there. But it doesn't matter what we've been through, we can be forgiven. We can start fresh by accepting the truth. Jesus Christ died for us! God raised Him from the grave to save us! Jesus lives to show us the right way! How awesome is that? God loves us unconditionally; flaws-n-all. He has given us a way out of all of our messes!

Psalms 86:8-17 reads:

> **For You, O Lord, are good, and ready to forgive [our trespasses, sending them away, letting them go completely and forever]; and You are abundant in mercy *and* love-kindness to all those who call upon You. (AMP)**

It's God's Will for all of His daughters to live eternally with Him, Jesus, and the Holy Spirit, together in His Heavenly Kingdom. (Rom. 6:23) The acceptance of Jesus opens your eyes (spiritually) to see the deceptive practices of the enemy. Just about everywhere you look things begin to take on a whole new understanding. But the greatest awareness of all,

Go Beyond Your Dreams
(Live Them!)

is when you begin to notice changes taking place within yourself. That's God reshaping the old you, filling your spirit, mind, body, and soul with more of a Christ-like image. This transitioning stage is the old you who once walked (lived) in darkness being filled (reborn) by the Holy Spirit!

In conclusion, whether you've ever craved a vision, a dream or both at once, they were imparted to you by God. All the earth is His, and the fullness thereof. Girlfriend, we belong to Him. God is solely responsible for planting those unique qualities inside of you. Your individuality is meant to glorify Him in everything that you do. Therefore, whatever you honestly enjoy doing (that thing that makes you giggle inside), is what you were born to do! A calm, peaceful spirit is one of the keys that can unlock the door to your destiny. God has not only equipped you with the right stuff to labor in your dreams, He has blessed you with the ability to birth them forth! Whether you realize it or not, anything you could ever possibly need to fulfill your visions has carefully been planted within your heart. Let me encourage you. Tap into your hidden treasures!

It's my desire that all of my readers make quality decisions concerning their visions and dreams. First and foremost, God is able to do exceeding abundantly above, and beyond anything you or I could ever ask, or think! (Eph. 3:20) Please do not be afraid to try. Don't prolong your destiny for another day. Girlfriend, don't forfeit your inheritance by choosing to ignore those God-given talents, ideas, visions, and dreams. God has a divine plan and purpose for you!

I challenge you to continue dreaming, and dream big! The only limitations preventing you from achieving the desires of your heart, are the limits you've placed on yourself. Girlfriend, stop wasting precious time. Become the conqueror of your dreams! Pursue what rightfully belongs to you. Prosperity in every area of your life doesn't have to be a dream you accept as being out of bounds. Your dream can become a reality!

May I suggest that you diligently exercise your heart (faith) everyday. Read God's Word to increase your faith. Talk about your vision/dream in the present. Then start expecting! Girlfriend, you were born for such a time as this! Abundant, successful, prosperous living can be yours, if you *really* want it! I dare you to go beyond your dreams, and live them!

Go Beyond Your Dreams
(Live Them!)

SALVATION (A MIRACLE) AWAITS YOU!

Focusing on self is the opposite of focusing on God. Anyone completely absorbed in self, ignores God, and ends up thinking more about self than God. That person ignores who God is and what He is doing. And God isn't pleased at being ignored.

But if God Himself has taken up residence in your life, you can hardly be thinking more of yourself than of Him. Anyone, of course, who has not welcomed this invisible but clearly present God, the Spirit of Christ, won't know what we're talking about. But for you who welcome Him, in who He dwells—even though you still experience all the limitations of sin—you yourself experience life on God's terms. It stands to reason, doesn't it, that if the alive-and-present God who raised Jesus from the dead moves into your life, He'll do the same thing in you that He did in Jesus, bringing you alive to Himself? When God lives and breathes in you (and He does, as surely as He did in Jesus), you are delivered from that dead life. With His Spirit living in you, your body will be as alive as Christ's!

So, don't you see that we don't owe this old do-it-yourself life one red cent? There's nothing in it for us, nothing at all. The best thing to do is give it a decent burial and get on with your new life. God's Spirit beckons. There are things to do and places to go! This resurrection life you received from God is not a timid, grave-tending life. It's adventurously expectant, greeting God with a childlike "What's next Papa?"

God's Spirit touches our spirits and confirms who we really are. We know who He is, and we know who we are: Father and children. And we know we are going to get what's coming to us—an unbelievable inheritance! We go through exactly what Christ went through. If we go through the hard times with Him, then we're certainly going to go through the good times with Him!

Romans 8:8-17 reads:

> **Those controlled by the sinful nature cannot please God. You, however, are controlled not by the sinful nature but by the Spirit, if the Spirit of God lives in you. And if anyone does not have the Spirit of Christ, he does not belong to Christ. But if Christ is in you, your body is dead because of sin, yet your spirit is alive because of righteousness. And if the Spirit of him who raised Jesus from the dead is living in you, he who raised Christ from the dead will also give life to your mortal bodies through his Spirit, who lives in you. Therefore, brothers, we have an obligation—but it is not to the sinful nature, to live according to it. For if**

Go Beyond Your Dreams
(Live Them!)

you live according to the sinful nature, you will die; but if by the Spirit you put to death the misdeeds of the body, you will live, because those who are led by the Spirit of God are sons of God. For you did not receive a spirit that makes you a slave again to fear, but you received the Spirit of sonship. And by him we cry, "Abba, Father." The Spirit himself testifies with our spirit that we are God's children. Now if we are children, then we are heirs—heirs of God and co-heirs with Christ, if indeed we share in his sufferings in order that we may also share in his glory. (THE MESSAGE)

Go Beyond Your Dreams

(Live Them!)

Go Beyond Your Dreams
(Live Them!)

ABBREVIATION REFERENCE
BOOKS OF THE BIBLE

Book/Chapter/Verse	Page
Deuteronomy 8:18	19
Ecclesiastes 5:9	26
Hebrews 11:6	28
John 10:10	28
Habakkuk 2:2	28
Matthew 9:20-22	33
Mark 5:24-34	33
Luke 8:43-48	33
I Peter 5:7	37
Romans 4:17	38
Habakkuk 2:3	42
Numbers 23:19	42
Habakkuk 2:2	43
Isaiah 40:8	43
Isaiah 55:11	44
Isaiah 41:10	52
II Corinthians 5:7	53
Psalms 37:4-5	60
Acts 3:8	61
Hebrews 10:35	62
Exodus 19:5	65
Exodus 15:24; 16:3; 17:3	65
III John 2	68
Proverbs 16:7	70
Jeremiah 15:11	70
James 3:5	75
Proverbs 18:21	75

Jeremiah 5:25	75
Psalms 39:1	76
Psalms 10:3-5	78
Deuteronomy 19:15	81
Acts 20:32	81
Deuteronomy 8:18	81
Deuteronomy 30:14	82
Romans 10:8	82
Job 15:5-6	85
Isaiah 55:8	85
I Corinthians 14:40	85
Psalms 149:2-5	86
Psalms 105:2; 135:1	87
Hebrews 13:5	92
Romans 8:37	93
Deuteronomy 15:6	94
Jeremiah 30:8	94
Deuteronomy 6:10-11; 19:8	94
Acts 13:23; 13:30	95
Jeremiah 33:6-9	95
Psalms 16:9	96
Isaiah 14:3	96
Psalms 84:11	97
Isaiah 55:11	98
Psalms 73:28; 86:10	104
Psalms 57:2	108
Psalms 119:81; 125:1; 30:5; 126:5	108
Psalms 145:14	109
Psalms 56:4; 56:10-11	110
Psalms 119:89	111
Philippians 4:13	111
I John 4:4	112
Psalms 18:32; 27:1	112
Hebrews 13:6	112
Genesis 18:4	112
Genesis 17:16	112

Go Beyond Your Dreams
(Live Them!)

Genesis 18:10-12	112
Hebrews 13:5	113
Genesis 21:1-2	115
Deuteronomy 14:2	116
Psalms 27:14	116
Psalms 9:9-10; 12:5-6	116
Isaiah 41:10	119
Romans 8:28-30	119
I Corinthians 10:13	120
Psalms 46:1; 54:4; 55:22	120
Deuteronomy 8:18	121
John 14:26	127
Ephesians 2:8	134
Psalms 55:22	135
I Peter 5:7	135
Psalms 37:4; 38:9	139
Deuteronomy 8:18	141
Proverbs 24:10	142
Hebrews 11:6	142
Romans 12:2	142
I Thessalonians 4:12	143
Psalms 34:19	143
Romans 10:17	143
John 15:7	143
James 1:22	144
II Corinthians 5:7	144
I Samuel 16:7	157
I Chronicles 28:9	157
Luke 6:45	158
Psalms 37:31	159
Psalms 90:8	159
Mark 4:22	159
Luke 8:17	159
II Corinthians 6:15	160
I Peter 5:8	161
Proverbs 21:2	165

Reference	Page
Psalms 121:2	168
Isaiah 26:3	168
I Peter 5:8	177
Luke 3:5	180
Philippians 4:7; 4:9	180
Colossians 3:15	180
I Corinthians 1:27	180
Hebrews 13:5	182
Psalms 33:20; 40:17; 70:5	182
Psalms 35:27	183
Nehemiah 8:8	183
Mark 4:37-39	184
Daniel 2:28-29	185
Isaiah 26:3	187
James 3:18	188
Proverbs 16:9	188
Philippians 4:13	190
Hebrews 8:12	195
Isaiah 44:2; 44:24	197
Ephesians 1:4	197
Psalms 139:14	197
Romans 6:23	198
Ephesians 3:20	199

Go Beyond Your Dreams
(Live Them!)

AUTHOR'S BIO

Farrell Ellis resides in Wilmington, Delaware where she is the front-desk receptionist at a law firm. She has been an active member of Spirit Life Ministries International Church for over ten years participating in both the Hospitality and Ushers/Greeters ministries. In the latter part of 2007, God gave her a vision for creating the *Spirit of Excellence* church newsletter, which she launched in January 2008.

Through God's Word, no matter what Farrell might envision, or dream, she has learned God is big enough to make the desires of her heart come to pass. Without question, she knows that God is able to do exceedingly above and beyond anything she could ever ask or think! Her debut book, *Go Beyond Your Dreams (Live Them!)* is certainly proof God is faithful to His Word.

For three years she repeatedly confessed Psalms 68:11 "The Lord gives the word [of power]; the women who bear and publish [the news] are a great host." (AMP) She not only confessed the words of that scripture, she allowed them to marinate within her heart until they became a living truth for her.

Farrell Ellis

Farrell Ellis firmly believes that the Word of God residing within a saturated faith-filled heart, spoken out of ones own mouth has the power to produce visions and dreams into becoming realities!

Go Beyond Your Dreams
(Live Them!)

To write or invite this great author for signings and motivational speaking engagements, please contact Farrell Ellis at:

farrellellis@comcast.net

www.ingramcontent.com/pod-product-compliance
Lightning Source LLC
Chambersburg PA
CBHW031245290426
44109CB00012B/441